# The Discovery of The Church

*A History of Disciple Ecclesiology*

By

WM. BARNETT BLAKEMORE

*The Reed Lectures for 1965*

Published by
REED AND COMPANY
Nashville, Tennessee

# CONTENTS

# PREFACE

For the Christian there are at least two great purposes in the study of history. The first of these purposes is to achieve that part of one's self-understanding which only history can provide. What we have been is not the definition of what we are, but we can never understand what we are apart from what we have been. For the Christian, the study of history is also a contribution to his understanding of God, for in Christian faith history has a Lord, and the Lord of history is God.

While no part of the story of man falls outside the history of salvation, it was particularly in the Jewish community before the birth of Jesus Christ, in the teachings and life of Jesus Christ, and in the history of the Church of Christ that the possibilities of both self-awareness and the understanding of God came to sharpest focus. History, especially biblical and church history, is inalienable from the study of divinity. Every step forward in historical studies is a step in the appropriation of God's revelation of himself. Therefore, the establishment of an historical lectureship is a matter of solemn and joyful moment for a religious communion.

The Forrest F. Reed Lectureship will both intensify and extend historical scholarship within the movements that descend from the work of Thomas and Alexander Campbell and Barton W. Stone. The morale for historical study will be intensified by the honor done for history in the establishment of this lectureship, adding to the dignity already bestowed upon historical scholarship by the existence of the Disciples of Christ Historical Society in which the lectureship is lodged. Historical scholarship will be extended through the topics for further studies inspired by this lectureship.

The initiation of such a lectureship is of such import that against the invitation to be the inaugural lecturer no demurrer may be entered. The only response can be that of obedience and one's best efforts to fulfill the terms of the lectureship. In that regard, from the outset, an unusual assistance was offered. The lecturer was assured full freedom, including the selection of topic, but it was indicated that, if desired, the Disciples of Christ Historical Society would seek to ascertain the topic which, at our moment in history, is of most concern to the Society's constituency. The research was carried out, and provided a topic so congenial to this lecturer that without hesitation the suggestion that this initial series deal with the doctrine of the church was accepted.

All who are associated with the Disciples of Christ Historical Society are greatly indebted to Mr. Forrest F. Reed of Nashville, Tennessee, for the faith and generosity with which he brought into existence the significant new platform of this lectureship established to enhance historical scholarship. To Dr. Willis R. Jones, President of the Disciples of Christ Historical Society, and to his staff, and to Dr. Hugh Riley of Louisville, Kentucky, chairman of the Lectureship Committee, I am especially grateful for ready assistance in the preparation of the lectures, and for their great hospitality during the time the lectures were being delivered in Nashville, Tennessee, November 8 and 9, 1965.

What emerges in the chapters of this book is something less than a full scale history of the doctrine of the church in the Campbell-Stone movement. It is rather an essay to follow two strands of the history of the Christian churches: their practical experience as churches, and their ideas about church. By God's grace such a study helps us to understand ourselves now as members of the Church of Christ upon earth, and in our discovery to find in part that obedience which, as churchmen, we should now fulfill.

Wm. Barnett Blakemore.

Disciples Divinity House,
Chicago, Illinois.
January 1, 1966

# INTRODUCTION

The chapters of this book have a parallel structure. This parallelism is not forced upon the historical material, but is imbedded in it, making it possible, in each of the three chapters to move from the concept of debate through the concept of discussion to the concept of dialogue.

Debate, discussion and dialogue can best be distinguished from each other in terms of the conclusions which are expected for each. In debate, at the outset there are two sides; it is expected that ultimately there will be a judgement selecting one side as the winner. Discussion does not require or even call for decision, especially in the area of doctrine; the objective of discussion is met if a congenial atmosphere is maintained, an atmosphere in which men may initiate and enhance practical co-operation—and keep the discussion going. In dialogue there are two sides which at the outset seem to be opposed; the expectation is that each of these is a variation upon the same truth, and that in dialogue there will emerge a new statement with which both parties to the dialogue will be able to identify. Dialogue does aim at doctrinal agreement.

The main topics of these chapters obviously do not exhaust the subject of the history of the doctrine of the church among the Christian Churches. They do illustrate how the Christian Churches, relating themselves to the Reformers, to the world, and to Rome in debate, discussion and dialogue, have moved forward in the discovery of the church.

# I

## Dialogue with the Reformers

In the city of Lexington, Kentucky, as the year 1832 began, there was initiated a unification into one movement of the Christian congregations of two predecessor movements. In the older of these movements the congregations called themselves Christian Churches, and their communion had come about not as they were acknowledged by some central organization, but as congregations recognizing their great similarities identified themselves with each other. These congregations were to be found on both sides of the Southern Appalachian Mountains, notably in the Carolinas and in Kentucky where, by 1832, their most beloved leader was Barton W. Stone. This movement had come to its initial focus in 1804 when a group of Presbyterian ministers who had a few months earlier established in central Kentucky a Springfield Presbytery, dissolved it and made their action known by publishing a "Last Will and Testament of the Springfield Presbytery." They urged the churches to take the name Christian and to establish a biblical faith and order "without any mixture of philosophy, vain deceit, traditions of men, or the rudiments of the world."[1]

The second movement, only slightly younger had begun in 1809 with the publication of "A Declaration and Address of the Christian Association of Washington, Pennsylvania." This document also called upon congregations to establish themselves in a biblical, or more precisely, a New Testament faith and order, rejecting human opinions and the inventions of men as of any authority.[2] The principles of this "Declaration and Address," written by Thomas Campbell,

9

had appealed to a number of Christians in the neighborhood of Washington, Pennsylvania. The movement launched by the document had existed first as a voluntary association of Christians, mainly Presbyterians, for church reformation; they called themselves variously "Reformers," "Disciples," "Christians," and later "Restorationists." Because these persons were no longer well received in their congregations, the movement existed as a small handful of churches in the neighborhood of Bethany, West Virginia, the home of Thomas Campbell's son, Alexander, who was rapidly becoming the leader of the movement. These few congregations soon allied themselves to the Baptist denomination and for seventeen uneasy years the movement existed within that context. It experienced considerable growth, notably in the Upper Ohio Valley. By 1830, those congregations which felt themselves to be part of this Reforming movement dissolved their association with the Baptists. Their leaders had already begun conversations with the congregations influenced by Barton W. Stone, conversations which were now intensified, looking toward the consolidation of the two movements. At the Lexington meetings which were the climax of these conversations there were no "elected representatives" and no written and formal "Basis of Union" or "Act of Union." The men present exercised a charismatic rather than an official leadership among the congregations. They had known each other for half a dozen years or more, and recognized that in their advocacy of "simple evangelical Christianity" they were much alike. They preached similar doctrine, worshipped in similar ways, and shared the same ethos. They discussed a number of points of faith and order, but nothing inhibited a growing accord, and a conviction that they were indeed one movement. Since the church polity which had developed in each group was strictly congregational, it was necessary for the leadership to persuade each congregation to understand itself in this new relationship. Virtually all of the churches of the Reformers under the leadership of the Campbells accepted this situation. So also did the great proportion of the Christian Churches under Barton W. Stone's influence, but the union was acknowledged by relatively few of the Christian churches east of the Appalachian mountains.

There is now no way of judging which of the two prior movements contributed the larger number of congregations and members to the new communion. The matter is of little moment however, for what did occur was an amalgamation of two traditions in such a manner that neither was lost, nor indeed was one subverted to the other even though shortly, because Thomas Campbell and Barton Stone were aging, the young and vigorous Alexander Campbell began to exercise a unique leadership which continued for several decades after the union was effected.

Why was the amalgamation so complete? The answer is not simple, in the sense that life is never simple. There was, of course, a wide agreement on specific items of doctrine, personal behavior, manner of worship and organization of the religious community, though an important element of the union was that all agreed that they were not concerned for a detailed conformity in matters of faith and practice, other than for those details which were expressly commanded by Scripture.[3] More important than the details was an accord with respect to several general principles. First, of course, was their common devotion to Jesus Christ as the Son of God and their savior. An immediate corollary was that all held the union of Christians to be one of their definite objectives. The view of the Bible which they held in common, and their common view of the nature of the Church are the two further most important general principles involved in the union, both of which must be examined in more detail.

With respect to the Bible, the *Last Will and Testament* and the *Declaration and Address* take identical positions.

The *Declaration and Address* states that the Christian Association will take all its measure "directly and immediately from the Divine Standard . . . without attempting to inculcate anything of human authority, of private opinion, or inventions of men."[4] The *Last Will and Testament* speaks of the Bible as "the only sure guide to heaven,"[5] without any competitor, providing "the simple gospel" to be preached "without any mixture of philosophy, vain deceit, traditions of men, or the rudiments of the world." Now while it is certainly true that these statements closely resemble hundreds of similar estimates of the Bible to be found throughout Protestantism, it must be remarked that these views agree in understanding the divinity which characterizes Holy Scripture as in no way consociated or associated with a human element. The Scriptures therefore stand above our mortality and error and are to be so handled that our humanity and the world do not become comingled with them. They are looked upon as containing a divinely revealed and sufficient guide to faith and practice, and this divine standard is the norm to which all men must repair for religious guidance. In these initial documents of the Christian churches there is, so far as the Bible is concerned a wall of separation between the divine and the human, and the Scriptures stand clearly and entirely on the divine side.

With respect to the church, the Declaration and Address and the Last Will and Testament reveal another striking identity. Both documents affirm the constitution of the church by God and not by men, and both speak in terms which imply an unbroken continuity of the church of Christ on earth since its constitution by God until now. This position is perhaps the more clearly stated in the famous first proposition of the Declaration and Address: "The Church of Christ on Earth is essentially, intentionally and constitutionally *one*; consisting of all those in every place that profess their faith in Christ and obedience to him in all things according to the Scriptures, and that manifest the same by their tempers and conduct."[6] In the Last Will and Testament, the relevant words are found in the Imprimis of the Testament: "We will that this body die, be dissolved, and sink into union with the body of Christ at large; for there is but one Body, and one spirit, even as we are called in one hope of our calling."[7] The position is elaborated in these further words from "The Witnesses' Address" appended by the six signators to the Last Will and Testament:

> At their last meeting they undertook to prepare a piece for the press entitled Observations on Church Government. . . . As they proceeded in their investigation they soon found neither precept nor example in the New Testament for such confederacies as modern Church sessions, Presbyteries, Synods, General Assemblies, etc. Hence they concluded that while they continued in that connection in which they then stood they were off the foundation of the Apostles and Prophets, of which Christ himself is the chief cornerstone. However just, therefore, their views of church government might have been, they would have gone out under the name and the sanction of a self-constituted body.[8]

Here then, with regard to the Church there emerges a position that is identical with that pertaining to the Scriptures. In her essence, the divinely constituted church is in no way comingled with our human nature. The signers of the Last Will and Testament acknowledged that in the conduct of their ministries they might personally err, but they sought to be in the connection that characterizes a church which is, to use Thomas Campbell's terms, divine in essence and constituted by God alone.

Furthermore, both these charter documents of the Christian churches are evidence that originally in these move-

ments there was more concern regarding the nature of
Christian community than there was over the Christian individual. To state it obviously, in both groups while all
asked the question, "What must we do to be saved?" more
important for them was the question, "What must we do to
be the Church of Christ?" or, to state the question again, "Is
the connection in which we now stand the church; if not,
in what connection will we be the church?" The primacy of
this question at the origins of the Christian churches has
often been obscured. That part of the movement which
originated in relation to the Cane Ridge Revival is so apt to
be identified with that particular camp meeting that it is
interpreted in terms of revivalistic sectarianism. Actually
the initial announcements of a meeting to be held at Cane
Ridge were for a "sacramental meeting," which might bring
men together as a community. It is indeed a complex matter to determine why a meeting called for purposes of
communion should have led into wide-sweeping experiences
of personal conversion. An insight from social psychology
would suggest that the latter were necessary to the former,
that the frontier could not become truly a community until
large numbers of men and women underwent personality
and character reconstructions that enabled a new community
to come into existence. If this is the case, it was in the
First Great Awakening that the diverse elements which had
poured into the North Atlantic seaboard were moulded into
the classical New England character, and the first consolidation of the mid-American character occurred in revivals of the Second Great Awakening. If so, even the
revivals, which seem to be a response to the question, "What
must I do to be saved," are a stage on the way to answering
the community question, "In what connection shall we stand
to be members of Christ's Church?"

In the work of the Campbells, the question about the
nature of the church is certainly primary. Her essential

oneness and its manifestation on earth; her organization
and her ministry; the qualifications both of her membership
and her officers; her ordinances—the meaning of her baptism
and the Lord's Supper which came to be placed at the center
of her worship as the Campbells interpreted it. Soon after
Thomas Campbell came to America, Presbyterians in Western Pennsylvania took issue with him on several grounds.
Although formal charges regarding Thomas Campbell's attitude toward openness in the communion service were
never pressed, his conduct regarding communion was sus-
pect. At about the same time his son Alexander in Scotland
wrestled with the issue of communion. The issue of communion is the issue of relationship together as church,
and the matter might have remained more to the forefront
of pre-occupation had not the arrival of Alexander Campbell's first child in 1812 precipitated the question of baptism.
While in this original appearance in the Campbell movement, the issue of baptism was related to the matter of
church membership, the decision for immersion and a long
association with the Baptists soon created an emphasis on
baptism in relation to personal salvation. Many in the
Campbell movement developed a pre-occupation with immersion, especially when influenced by the preaching of
Walter Scott. The waning of Walter Scott's leadership
after the dissolution of the Mahoning Association and the
Union of 1832 is in part attributable to his inability to
comprehend, as Campbell could, the problems of religious
community. Even so, though Campbell taught that the
membership of the church consists of immersed believers,
his dominant teaching with respect to baptism is that it is
for the remission of sins. This way of interpreting baptism
primarily in terms of personal salvation remains the standard
Disciple teaching until well into the twentieth century. Only
then do we begin to see a swing toward a primary emphasis
once again on baptism in terms of its connection to the

Christian community.

What happened to the question, "What must we do to be the Church of Christ?" After the Union of 1832 the question dies away. The congregations had worked through to practical agreement on various details of worship, and the great general answer was adopted: The Divine Standard provides us with a guide to church order on which all Christians can unite. This order was asserted to be congregational in character, called for the immersion of believers as the form of baptism, the weekly observance of the Lord's Supper, and abolished clerical and sacerdotal concepts in favor of a ministry defined strictly in terms of the local congregation and lay qualifications. With this understanding of the church the Christian Churches moved with the frontier and experienced a marked success. Denominations with clerical concepts of the ministry in terms of high educational levels or sacerdotal identification often could not provide an adequate religious ministry to the burgeoning frontier. In this ministerial vacuum, the frontiersmen took hold of the concepts of the Baptist, Christian or Methodist churches and themselves established congregations throughout mid-America and across the Rockies to the Pacific shore. The assumption by the frontier layman of congregational ministries as defined in the Christian churches was no vast step beyond the non-congregational ministries which the rigors of frontier life had forced upon him. Not only did many a man on the frontier discover that if there was to be any experience of worship and devotions for his family he would have to provide it. Frontier life also required that many a body be laid to rest without benefit of clergy. Many a man and wife, when a child had perished, knew whatever comfort came from no other man of God than a neighbor farmer, and many a frontier farmer had himself been to his neighbor the only minister to the neighbor's grief. It was but a step from these ministries to serving in congregational

ministries defined in terms of ordinances, and the frontiersmen took the step. The frontier produced a striking type
of personality in the preacher farmer who plowed a hard
ground, and knew that men hardened by such ploughing
required the convictions of a strong religious discipline if
they were to build their community. The type is well portrayed by Vachel Lindsay:

> *Into the acres of the new-born state,*
> *He poured his strength, and plowed his ancient name,*
> *And, when the traders followed him, he stood*
> *Towering above their furtive souls and tame.*
>
> *He read by night, and built his world by day.*
> *The farm and house of God to him were one.*
> *For forty years he plowed and preached and wrought—*
> *A statesman in the fields who bent to none.*
>
> *His plowmen neighbors were as lords to him.*
> *His was an ironside, democratic pride.*
> *He served a rigid Christ, but served him well—*
> *And, for a lifetime, saved the countryside.*
>
> *And many a sturdy grandchild bears his name*
> *In reverence spoken, till he feels akin*
> *To all the lioneyed who build the world—*
> *And lion dreams begin to burn within.*[9]

This frontier religion also confirmed the concept of the
ministerial self-sufficiency of the local congregation, and this
confirmation the Christian Churches in all their parts—
Church of Christ, Disciples of Christ, Independent, and so
on—have not forgotten.

The most recent general history of the Christian Church
to come from a Disciple is *The Church and Its Culture* by
R. M. Pope, professor of Church History at Lexington
Theological Seminary.[10] At the outset of his book, Dr. Pope
defines the church in terms of the gathering together of two
or three in Christ's name. In lyrical prose, Dr. Pope de-

scribes a simple service of communion held on a Western
Pacific island in the last months of the Second World War.
Only a few men are present, and they come from different
denominations. When Dr. Pope asks, "Was this an instance
of the church?" no one of Christian conscience could answer
"No," yet the way in which the question is set up in the
first place was learned by Dr. Pope from that Christian
Church definition of church in terms of the ministerially
self-sufficient congregation of the frontier—a type of congregation only rarely seen since frontier times except under
the extreme exigencies of the battle-line, itself a type of
frontier situation.

As the frontier passed by, the congregations of Christian
Churches began to do something more than establish themselves as worshipping congregations. They availed themselves of means of communication with each other, means
which were originally provided for them by their charismatic
leaders. During the 1830s they moved under this leadership
to the establishment of area home missionary societies and,
soon after, of educational institutions. They established
some identity of worship by using hymnals and Bible versions provided by the leadership. They supported Bible
societies and other non-denominational enterprises (though
as a rule only if the leadership endorsed them). Furthermore, they began to develop a professional ministry which
provided settled pastoral care and preaching to the congregations. By the 1840s members of the congregations
began to form those "societies" and organizations which
would be the successors to the enterprises that had been
personally provided and supervised by charismatic leaders.
The story of D. S. Burnet (who has suffered an "Undeserved
Obscurity" and whose excellent biography by Dr. Noel L.
Keith[11] has almost suffered a similar fate), is central to this
stage of the development of the Christian Churches. Almost
from the beginning of this organizational development,

Alexander Campbell was aware that it involved an ambiguity. The strictly congregationalist polity which the early leadership of the movement had endorsed left the implication that all this burgeoning organizational life, however worthy, was not part of the church. Indeed, one stream of the Campbell heritage to this day would even assert that such organizations beyond the local congregation ought not come into existence. Others would acknowledge their right to exist, though their congregational polity provides no principles by which congregations may exercise over these organizations a restraint of abuses of the congregations into which the organizations may from time to time fall.[12] Alexander Campbell and Barton Stone were aware of the problem. A. T. DeGroot in *The Nature of the Church*, 1961, wrote:

> A neglected chapter in our brotherhood history is the occasional efforts on the part of both Stone and Campbell to induce the brethren to adopt certain measures and practices of Presbyterianism in the inter-congregational life of the churches. An article in the *British Millennial Harbinger* for 1854 said that in addition to the congregational element seen in the church as disclosed in the New Testament "there is also a presbyterian element and an episcopal element." As Leslie L. Kingsbury says, "It is clear that Campbell would have preferred a form which had a combination of congregational and presbyterian features, but the movement spread so rapidly it eventually took a congregational form."[13]

Chapter XXIV, "The Body of Christ," in Alexander Campbell's *Christian System*[14] largely supports the view put forward by Dr. Kingsbury. This chapter was written in the late 1830s and it is a clarion call for cooperation between the churches, asserting that such cooperation is of the very essence of the Christian institution, though the manner of cooperation is left to the churches to decide in terms of their objectives and the circumstances under which they exist. Whether or not Alexander Campbell, perhaps in the 1840s, might have been able to persuade his followers that there were some things to be learned from Presbyterianism, he was shortly caught up into an enterprise which was to become his most extensive and influential definition of the distinctions between Presbyterianism and his own movement. This enterprise was the last and longest of his five debates.[15] It took place in November, 1843, in Lexington, Kentucky. The Presbyterian point of view was represented by Dr. N. L. Rice, a minister of Paris, Kentucky.

It is fair to state that in an age which did not yet know the term "adult education" because little of it existed, public debates, especially when done by skilled debaters, were occasions of great adult education—and by the 1840s Mr. Campbell had become a truly great debater. He had a skillful opponent in Mr. Rice. This debate was, throughout its sixteen days, a lively occasion which drew great audiences. Evidently each side thought it had won the debate, but subsequently there were second thoughts on both sides. Ensuing relations between the debaters were bitter. The Presbyterians soon sold their publication rights to Disciple interests. It may still be asked whether the debate should ever have been held. There are Christian Church members who have prized Mr. Campbell's work on this debate as the greatest single enterprise that he ever undertook on behalf of his followers. Others feel the results of the debate were deplorable. It must be admitted that this debate provided both Presbyterians and Christians with very clear expositions of their distinction from each other. The wording of the six topics for the debate sometimes led Campbell to emphasize the negative and iconoclastic elements of an issue on which he had in recent years been developing more positive emphases. In this debate, one steps backward in time from the edifying moods of the *Millennial Harbinger* toward the polemic of the *Christian Baptist* days. The first topic for debate was that, "Immersion in water of a proper subject is the one only Apostolic or Christian baptism." Mr. Campbell made many converts to his position and, between sessions, immersed them. The second stage of the debate was an affirmation by Mr. Rice that the infant of believing parents is a scriptural subject of baptism; the third topic was that Christian baptism is for the remission of past sins. Mr. Campbell's position on these topics inevitably led him to re-emphasize the individual and led him away from any reconsideration of the definition of baptism primarily in terms of Christian community. The fourth topic was Mr. Rice's affirmation that baptism should be administered only by a bishop or ordained presbyter. Mr. Rice took a very curious approach. Instead of arguing positively to the topic he argued negatively against the idea of lay baptism, insisting that this doctrine had arisen because Mr. Campbell having adopted the false doctrine of baptismal regeneration, had to make baptism available at any hour of the day or night. Alexander Campbell saw his opportunity, marched to good Presbyterian land and occupied it, but with a twist which, echoing the frontier experience, gave comfort to the anti-clerical tendencies in the Christian Churches. Here are Campbell's words:

Where there is no church, but disciples of Christ scattered abroad, not organized, there can be no offices. When then anyone desires baptism, any one to whom he applies may administer it. When a few brethren in one family, or neighborhood, organize themselves to meet once a week to show forth the Lord's death, to read the Scriptures, sing and pray together, having no ordained officer among them, they appoint one of themselves to break "the loaf of blessings" and to distribute the "cup of salvation." All this the New Testament, reason, common sense approve. But when societies are formed, Christian communities created, and a church organization established by agreement, then indeed all officers are filled by the voice and ordination of the people. When that is accomplished, no one has the right, either inherent, natural or divine, to discharge social duties, without a call and appointment from his compeers and associates. Do not Presbyterians, sensible, intelligent Presbyterians assent to these views? I sincerely think they do. They have no faith in the doctrine of hereditary grace—of official power transmitted from age to age, through the leaky and crazy corporations of human bodies.

The fifth proposition dealt with the working of the Holy Spirit in conversion and sanctification. Here Mr. Campbell represented again the kind of doctrine found originally in essays in the *Christian Baptist*. This doctrine reduces the present activity of the Holy Spirit to the strengthening of morality in individual persons and the enhancement of fervor in individual preachers. Campbell's doctrine of the Holy Spirit in relation to the church will receive more attention in the third chapter of this series. (See footnote 71.)

The final point of the debate in its positive aspect was an assertion by Mr. Campbell that personal committment to Christ is the only requisite to membership in his church, and therefore is the ground of Christian unity. In the debate however, the argument proceeded in terms of the heretical nature and schismatic effects of creeds, confirming into an anti-creedalism the distinterest of the Christian Churches in theological and confessional symbols.

Never again in his life would Mr. Campbell produce as a single unit of work anything comparable to this debate which ran to over half a million words. It is difficult, at this distance, not to put a negative estimate upon the debate's significance, at least so far as the doctrine of the church is concerned. Everything that was being said in the debate was being said over against pedo-baptism in general and Presbyterianism in particular; nothing was being said in the light of the now rapidly developing structural life of the Christian Churches, nothing regarding the nature of the Church which pushed beyond the doctrines which had emerged with the Union of 1832. If anything, the debate tended to confirm the members of the Christian Churches in what were already becoming their prejudices, one of which was that they were markedly different from Presbyterianism. What was happening was that point by point distinctions between the Christian Churches and Presbyterianism were being drawn. Therefore the common patrimony of the Christian Churches and American Presbyterianism in the rich heritage of Puritan emphasis on the Bible and in the Swiss and Calvinist Reform became more and more obscured. Convinced that they were uniquely succeeding in returning to New Testament Christianity "without any mixture of philosophy, vain deceit, traditions of men, or the rudiments of the world," and "without attempting to inculcate anything of human authority, or private opinion, or inventions of men," they were particularly blind to their derivation from the same general context as those very Presbyterians against whom they argued most strongly. The fact that Mr. Campbell's debate with N. L. Rice was both his most extended and most unpleasant in the sequel confirmed Campbell's followers in their prejudice against Presbyterianism.

It is in the broad sweep of history that it is possible to discern that within Protestantism there are four or five major divisions: Lutheranism, Episcopalianism, the Reformed Churches, all of which have always had as much or more concern for the Christian community as for the Christian individual, and a group including the Anabaptists,

Pietists and Pentecostals in which emphasis falls mainly on the Christian individual. When Protestantism is so analyzed, it is obvious where the Christian Churches belong. They are in the family of the Reformed Churches, and as we shall see a little later, they are currently returning to a strong consciousness that this is the case.

Fortunately, so deeply ingrained into the spirit of the Christian Churches was their concern for the unity of Christians, that though they may have debated sharply with other Christians, they did not separate themselves from them, but established a variety of cooperative relationships. Some members of the Christian Churches objected, but virtually all followed the suggestions of Mr. Campbell that the work of Bible societies should be supported. The rise of the Sunday School movement, Christian Endeavor, evangelistic societies, and of national boards for interdenominational activities in a variety of areas all came after the death of Mr. Campbell, but these movements were joined by the great majority of Christian Churches. At the same time, there were some who were sensitive to the fact that all of these activities went beyond anything contemplated in the original ecclesiology of the Christian Churches, and who therefore withheld or withdrew from these cooperative enterprises. The Church of Christ which emerged as a distinct entity in 1906 defined itself in part in terms of a strict congregational doctrine which could allow no organization beyond the local congregations. Meanwhile, the Christian Churches went on with those practical developments for which in theory they lacked clear justification, and for which they had no theory of the church that provided significant guidance in the development of organization. But where consciousness was not clear, conscience was insistent. Not only did they organize among themselves for missionary, benevolent and educational purposes, but the impulse to Christian unity was so great that by means of a special convention there were Disciples of Christ present as appointed delegates at the chartering of the Federal Council of Churches in 1908. Disciples of Christ have been charter members at every stage of the development of the twentieth century ecumenical movement.

As we shall see presently, by 1900 the conception of the Bible which had emerged in the Union of 1832 was already undergoing transformation. It is remarkable that leaders in the Christian Churches were still employing the 1832 conception of the church in their growing ecumenical relations. Actually the time of change was at hand, but as late as 1916, the original Disciple conception of the church was seriously and earnestly put forth by a scholarly leader as the way to achieve Christian union. We must however count this work of Frederick D. Kershner in his book entitled *How to Promote Christian Union* as the last significant attempt to plead within the context of the ecumenical movement what we have been calling the 1832 concept of the church.[16] Dr. Kershner's book is required reading for anyone who wants to understand the ecclesiological situation of the Christian Churches. In one sense it marks the end of an era in so far as it reproduces unaltered the traditional Christian Church concept of the church. In another sense it points to the future in its revelation of how deeply involved in and familiar with every aspect of the dawning ecumenical movement was the leadership of the Christian Churches in the early years of this century.[17]

The inadequacies of the strictly congregational polity of the earliest Disciple ecclesiology were long in coming to the consciousness of the Disciples. This is the more remarkable when it is recognized that the original concept of the Bible began to be modified almost as soon as it was formed. Because of the singular place of authority which he and his followers gave to the New Testament, Alexander Campbell early felt the need for a new version. His motivation for engaging in the production of a new version, as indicated in his preface to it in 1826, was that a living language is always changing, and therefore the Bible to remain comprehensible must constantly be revised in terms of contemporary speech.[18] A decade later, in connection with the first edition of *The Christian System*, 1835, he was acknowledging also that biblical literature could not be understood without taking into account certain circumstances of its origins.[19] In that connection he published seven rules of interpretation of the Bible. These rules involve the historical circumstances under which the book was written, the author and the dispensation within which he speaks, philological principles regarding common usage and the strict identification of tropical language, and the principle of "the understanding distance," a tantalizing term whose meaning Alexander Campbell did not develop. These principles endorsed by Campbell have long been recognized as "lower or textual" criticism. It is not the purpose of these lectures to deal with Christian Church doctrine about the Bible except as it effects the doctrine of the church. We do not need to detail the rise of the higher criticism, the sharpness of debate between the more fundamentalist and the more modernist elements within the communion, nor the continuing interest of Christian Church scholarship in the problem of biblical interpretation. Suffice it to say that in our own day this concern has been carried forward by such able men as Jack Finegan and the late C. K. Thomas. In the work of the Panel of Scholars (1955-63) the problem of biblical authority was a major concern of all to which J. Philip Hyatt, William R. Baird, Stephen J. England, Dwight E. Stevenson and others contributed papers.[20] It continues as a special concern for these men and such scholars as Glenn Rose and Jack Suggs. Some of these men exercise their concern through the Commission on Theology and Unity of the Department of Studies of the Council on

Christian Unity, this Commission being the unit within the Christian Churches at the present time which most self-consciously carries responsibility for problems of biblical interpretation and authority. What was becoming clear early in this century was that an exclusive biblical support could no longer be claimed by a strictly congregationalist polity. This position was acknowledged in 1938 at the Denver Assembly of the International Convention, by Frederick D. Kershner, then Dean of the School of Religion of Butler University, in his presidential address to the convention in which he spoke of the varieties of church polity present in the churches of the New Testament era.

During the years of the Second World War and thereafter in response to circumstances both in America and abroad, the Christian Churches experienced another stage of organizational development. Cooperation in communion-wide planning emerged, first on a temporary basis, for a Crusade for a Christian World in the 1940s. As the decade of the 1950's began, a Council of Agencies was formed. A Home and State Missions Planning Council effected joint planning in the important area of establishing and enhancing congregations in America. Such developments inevitably increased the responsibilities of many men involved in general services to the churches, particularly of state secretaries. The formation of the World Council of Churches in 1948 was the harbinger of an increased ecumenical activity including more serious conversations with other communions regarding the possibilities of union. In these ecumenical discussions, representatives of the Christian Churches have found themselves increasingly in need of new understandings of the way in which their own communion conceives the church. Obviously the Christian Churches have long since outgrown their traditional congregational polity, though these organizational developments have not, in the eyes of most, resulted in any

abridgement of the fundamental rights of local congregations. However by the 1950s many were beginning to ask,
"What are the fundamental rights of congregations, and
how are we to understand the connections in which we now
stand?" During the 1950s these queries were frequently
voiced by the question, "What is our doctrine of the
church?" This question began to be heard more and more
frequently, and to be asked with more and more urgency.
Now in the mid 1960s the Christian Churches are more
deeply involved in again asking the question, "What must
we do to be a church of Christ?" than at any time since
1832. A renewed consciousness of the church as a topic of
special concern has been arising. What has happened is
that the Christian Churches have discovered that they cannot proceed forever in a purely practical or pragmatic way,
and that at last the doctrinal questions relevant to practice
must be raised. This need came to sharp focus early in the
1960s with the establishment of a Commission for Brotherhood Restructure. The Commission has stated that it was
brought into existence because the Christian Churches were:
"Inspired by a heritage of mutual accomplishment and
fellowship, chastened by weaknesses and failures, prompted
by growing insights into the meaning of scripture, the
nature of the church and a widening ecumenical vision;
troubled by the complexity of structures within the congregation, in state and national conventions, in boards, agencies
and institutions, and in their relationships; challenged by a
growing awareness of world needs; and sensitive to the
insistent demands of the times." In responding to this complex of motivations, the Commission soon discovered that
it could not effect a meaningful restructure without pushing
forward to a definition of the church which would (1) take
into account the organizational developments of over a century, either to judge, confirm, or improve them, and which
would (2) be part of a renewal of the spirit of the churches.

Restructure within and ecumenical involvement without have alike precipitated the need for a restatement by the Christian Churches of their understanding of the nature of the Church. This new understanding is at the present time in formation. Contributions are coming to it from several strands of thought among the Christian Churches in earlier years of this century, and through current dialogue with the Roman Catholic Church, with the world, and with the churches of the Reformation. The concluding section of this chapter deals with ideas emergent in the current dialogue of Disciples of Christ with other Reformed bodies.

One strand of the new consciousness of the church as a special concern is to be seen in the shift that has taken place in this century regarding the interpretations of baptism. In the 19th century the design of baptism was, in the Christian churches, universally said to be the remission of sins. In 1914, there appeared from the pen of Dr. Charles Clayton Morrison of Chicago a book which made what is perhaps the earliest break with this tradition in favor of defining baptism primarily in terms of an initiation or entrance into the Christian community.[21] The 1914 book, entitled *The Meaning of Baptism* was written because Dr. Morrison had come to understand that far from promoting Christian Union, the traditional Christian Church doctrine of baptism was a hindrance.[22] He realized that the Christian Churches needed to re-examine their understanding of baptism. His definition of the meaning of baptism represents a shift from pre-occupation with personal salvation to concern for the character of Christian community. Only gradually have others among the Christian Churches come to the point where they put the emphasis regarding baptism primarily on its character as the way of entry into the Christian communion. In 1955, baptism was the topic of one of the study breakfast groups at the Toronto Assembly of the World Convention of Churches of Christ. In the pamphlet issued in 1956 on the basis of the discussions of that study group, two meanings were given to baptism. First it is interpreted in terms of repentance and submission to God on the part of the submissive sinner. Then a second interpretation, full of church consciousness was given.

> Baptism is also the experience of one who yields his life to Christ in trust and obedience. The new birth and the death, burial and resurrection of the believer also describes the entrance of the convert into the church, the body of Christ. These are, in reality, one and the same event, the entrance into new life and the entrance into the fellowship with members of the church. The church is of such a spiritual nature that rather than join it one must be born into it, and as the church realizes its true nature, the life within its fellowship is in such contrast to that outside that it is said, "We have passed out of death into life." (I John 3:14)[23]

In 1960, Association Press published *First Steps in Theology* by Dr. Jack Finegan, Christian Church minister of Berkeley, California. In the chapter on the church, Dr. Finegan defines the church as the Household of Faith. "Whether or not Jesus self-consciously intended to found a church, he definitely intended to call together a new group of people, to launch a new program and to give a new promise. This new people with a mission and a destiny were to be a household of faith." Baptism is then defined as the ceremony of introduction to this group, and the Lord's Supper as the ceremony of fellowship within the group.[24]

In a paper on "The Origin and Meaning of Christian Baptism" presented to the Panel of Scholars, J. Philip Hyatt of Nashville, Tennessee presents four meanings associated with Early Christian baptism, the first of which is:

Baptism was a rite of initiation into a community—at first

an eschatological community, later the church as the body of Christ.[25]

The other three meanings connect baptism with repentance and forgiveness, with the concept of death and resurrection, and with the gifts of the Holy Spirit. The important point is that Dr. Hyatt mentions initiation into the community first, and in the later section of his paper as he discusses positive meanings of baptism today there is strong emphasis on the connection between baptism and the Christian community: "by baptism the church receives the believer into the covenant community, to surround him with its warm fellowship . . . in baptism the believer and the church both witness to Christ."[26]

In 1962 the first volume in the Christian Discipleship Series, a new curriculum for adults in the Christian Churches, appeared. This first study course, written by Dr. Dwight E. Stevenson, is on "The Church—What and Why?" Chapter five discusses Christian Baptism, and Dr. Stevenson presents three meanings: admission into the church, a presentation of the gospel in the death, burial and resurrection symbolism, and the symbol of personal conversion.[27] Significantly it is admission into the church that is put first. This recognition of baptism as admission into the church enables Dr. Stevenson to clarify the problem of rebaptism. "Since baptism is the door into the believing community, it follows that it is a rite performed only once in the life of each Christian. It does not need to be repeated. In this respect it is like a wedding ceremony in relation to marriage."[28]

The final section of this chapter will deal briefly with the rediscovery by the Christian Churches of their affinity with the churches of the Calvinist-Swiss Reform, and what this rediscovery means for the correction of the anti-clerical bias in the traditional Christian Church understanding of ministry in association with the church. Since 1830 when the followers of Alexander Campbell and Walter Scott completed their withdrawal from Baptist association, conversations looking toward a reunion have periodically sprung up between Baptists and Disciples. The common practice of immersion seems ever to indicate that there must be great similarity between these two groups—but always the conversations collapse, just as the original union did. There has recently been a growing feeling among representatives of the Christian Churches that the real issue is that Baptist consciousness centers on the religious competency of the individual, whereas for the Christian Churches the center of consciousness is the Christian community. In the past two decades, as conversations with the Baptists have dwindled, Christian Church conversations with groups stemming from the Calvinist Reform have intensified. The Christian Churches are at present involved officially in Conversations with the United Church of Christ which incorporates the majority of former Congregationalists, and with the Consultation on Church Unity which includes the Presbyterians as well as the United Church of Christ and several other denominations. In these conversations, the crucial issue has turned out to be, not the difference of mode of baptism, but the nature of ministry. What has happened is that representatives of the Christian Churches have had to face the fact that whereas traditionally they have defined ministry in terms of the ministerial self-sufficiency of the local congregation, in practice they have erected a professional ministry that serves not only in the pastoral leadership of congregations, but provides leadership at more general levels of organization within the Christian community. Because their later leaders have been, in terms of traditional Christian Church thought, theoretically denied any ministerial standing they are vulnerable to development in terms of secularized bureaucracy. This danger was pointed out in 1954 in lectures given on the Christian Foundation Lectureship at the College of the Churches of Christ at the University of Toronto.[29] At the same time that the Christian Churches have had to confront the shortcomings of their tendency to generalize the frontier situation and its discovery of the religious self-sufficiency of congregations, the parties to both the Conversations and the Consultations have had to confront their failure to recognize that sufficiency at all. As a result they have tended toward a professionalism in the ministry which has shrivelled the efficacy for spiritual leadership on the part of the membership of the local congregation.

The Christian Churches have at last come into dialogue with the Reformers. A century and a half ago, the pages of the *Christian Baptist* resounded with descriptions of what Alexander Campbell called the "kingdom of the clergy" which he believed validated a radical anti-clericalism. A few years later in his *Christian System,* Campbell wrote a chapter on the Christian ministry in which he propounded a three level order of the ministry. Except for the fact that Campbell placed this whole order within the local congregation it owes far more to Presbyterianism than to any other source—including the New Testament. But both Campbell and his followers were so eager to define themselves over against Presbyterianism that they could not then understand the source of their ideas about ministry. Nor did the followers of either Stone or Campbell realize that the typical worship which their congregations followed was certainly derived from the *Directories* for worship of the Reformed cities of Geneva and Edinburgh. The Christian Churches in 1832 thought they were duplicating primitive Christian worship. Today it is difficult to believe that in recent centuries any group has had the information that would be necessary to recreate with any great degree of fidelity the worship forms of primitive Christianity. Certainly Zwingli thought that was what he was doing on that Easter Sunday in 1523 when the communion elements were carried by deacons to the congregation sitting in the pews. Zwingli proclaimed that on that day the biblical procedure was restored. Nowadays we know that whatever the New Testament procedure was it did not involve deacons carrying the elements to a congregation sitting in pews.

Fortunately in our day the debate with the Reformers, typified in Mr. Campbell's encounter with Mr. Rice has been superseded by dialogue with the Reformers. In debate, there are two sides, and a presupposition that one side is right. In dialogue also there are two sides at the outset, but the presupposition is not that either side is right—but that there is a truth to be discovered which incorporates whatever is right on each side and transcends both in a new understanding.

In dialogue with the Reformers, a definition of order of the Christian ministry is emerging. This definition is really new to all communions in the dialogue. Disciples of Christ in the Consultation and in the Conversations, true to what is valid in their frontier heritage, have found themselves arguing for the conduct of the Lord's Supper by the eldership, congregationally conceived. The report is that to this conception, the other parties of the dialogue listen as to something refreshing, not unaware that it has more relationship to their own denominational traditions, as well as some relationship to Scripture, a relationship which needs a renewed examination. Others in the dialogue with the Reformers, true to what is valid in their experience, argue for a pastoral office more general than that of the pastor to the local congregation. Sometimes this more general pastorate is argued in terms of episcopacy, sometimes in terms of presbytery, sometimes in terms of a combination of these two historic forms of general oversight.

In 1965, another meeting was held at Cane Ridge Meeting

House. This meeting like that of 1803 was a "sacramental meeting." At the 1965 meeting those present were members of the communions in the Consultation, and observers of other communions. The Lord's Supper was celebrated with lay elders ministering at the Table. This 1965 and second sacramental meeting at Cane Ridge is as full of meaning about the church as was that first sacramental meeting in 1803—and, in the end, may also be as significant historically.

## II

### *Dialogue with the World*

The student of the early history of the Christian Churches in relationship to the world about them finds himself facing an interesting dilemma. Face to face with their world, these 19th century American Disciples were decidedly ambivalent. At one moment they are full of immediate and practical intention to bring about the Kingdom of God on earth. At another moment they hold themselves strongly and critically aloof from the world. Let us notice first some of their acceptance of their world.

There is no doubt that the American national situation of the first decade of the last century had a powerful positive effect upon the spirits and the imagination of the leadership of the new movement. Thomas Campbell had lived into his forties on the British Isles without achieving either good health or finding a satisfying religious context. Like many another of his countrymen he felt the lure of the new nation to the west across the Atlantic. In America, Thomas Campbell was soon filled with the sense of a new start in life, not only for himself and his family, but for communities, not only in their political life but also in their religious organization. In the years of his ministry in Ireland, Thomas Campbell had been deeply disturbed by the multiplicity of sectarian divisions, and in the years 1804 and 1805 he gave leadership to an effort for the unification of the Burgher and Anti-Burgher Presbyterian Churches in Ireland. The attempt failed, though the union did occur in 1820 after Mr. Campbell had removed to America. The story of this effort at reunification can be read in *Thomas Campbell: Man of the Book* by Dr. Lester McAllister of Christian Theological Seminary.[30] For the history of our Christian Churches this experience was for Mr. Campbell a significant preparation for the work which he launched in America in 1809 with a different degree of success. It is instructive to compare the documents of 1804-05 with *The Declaration and Address*. The latter continues the former's literary style and use of formal construction around propositions, but there is also something very different in the latter, particularly in its vigorous tone and clarity of objective. Much of the difference is attributable to the new American context in which Thomas Campbell wrote the *Declaration and Address*. There is every reason to believe that when Thomas Campbell entitled his writing *A Declaration and Address* he had in mind the Declaration of Independence. He realized, that he was seeking to effect in the religious sphere something comparable to the achievement of America's political forefathers in the political sphere. In both instances the problem was to find the ground upon which many might become one. *The Declaration and Address* like the Declaration of Independence opens with the apologetic for the action announced in the declaration.

From the series of events which have taken place in the churches for many years past, especially in this western country, as well as from what we know in general in the present state of things in the Christian world; we are persuaded that it is high time for us not only to think, but also to act, for ourselves, to see with our own eyes, and to take all our measures directly and immediately from the *Divine Standard*: to this alone we feel ourselves divinely bound to be conformed; as by this alone we must be judged.[31]

In the mind of Thomas Campbell "this western country"

presented its Christian community with an opportunity so great and unique that it could be accepted only as a challenge. Thomas Campbell was enough of a Calvinist that he would not in blind optimism assert that rising to meet the challenge meant that the challenge would be met. Events certainly belong to God, he said, but duty belongs to us, and our duty obviously is to respond to the particular opportunity of the American scene, which by its contrast with other parts of the world is unique.

> The favorable opportunity which Divine Providence has put into your hands in this happy country, for the accomplishment of so great a good, is in itself, a consideration of no small encouragement. A country happily exempted from the baneful influence of a civil establishment of any particular form of Christianity—from under the direct influence of the anti-Christian hierarchy—and at the same time, from any formal connexion with the devoted nations, that have given their strength and power unto the beast; in which, of course, no adequate reformation can be accomplished, until the word of God is fulfilled and the vials of his wrath poured out upon them. Happy exemption indeed, from being the object of such awful judgments. Can the Lord expect or require anything less from a people in such unhampered circumstances—from a people so liberally furnished with all means and mercies, than a thorough reformation, in all things civil and religious, according to his word.[32]

Set over against this attraction to the American scene was Campbell's abhorrence of divisions among Christians. The second paragraph of the *Address* is too long to repeat but its topic sentence and introductory passage deserve to be read:

> What awful, and distressing effects have those sad di-

visions produced! What adversions, what reproaches, what backbitings, what excommunications and even persecutions . . . and this must continue to be the case as long as those schisms exist, for, as says the Apostle, where envying and strife is, there is confusion and every evil work. What dreary effects of these accursed divisions are to be seen, even in this highly favored country, where the sword of the civil magistrate has not as yet learned to serve at the altar. Have we not seen congregations broken to pieces, neighborhoods of professing Christians first thrown into confusion by party contentions, and, in the end entirely deprived of gospel ordinances; while, in the meantime, large settlements and tracts of country remain to this day utterly destitute of a gospel ministry; many of them in little better than a state of heathenism; the churches being either so weakened with divisions that they cannot send them ministers; or the people so divided among themselves, that they will not receive them.[33]

Just as the political leaders of early America abhorred political factions and sought to work out for the new nation a government in which factionalism would be overcome in a transcendant national unity, so the religious leaders of the Disciples abhorred religious division and sought to discover the way in which religious sectarianism could be overcome. They found the answer in a concept of church membership which was inclusive of any who professed themeselves Christians. Believing that they were possessed of the key that solved the difficult problem of sectarian strife, they had a spiritual release which at times amounted to a euphoria which spilled over into areas other than the ecclesiastical. For instance, in his book on the *Messiahship*, Walter Scott indulges in praise of the American polticial system in terms that imply a divine sanction for the American form of government. His attitude in this regard is far less restrained than that of Campbell, as shall be indicated in a few moments.

In 19th century America there was not only a great deal of optimism regarding political institutions, but by mid-century the optimistic attitude was beginning to be enhanced by another element—namely scientific and technological advance. The communion of Christian Churches did not resist this new element in man's intellectual development. Their first educational institution established in 1836 at Georgetown, Kentucky was named Bacon College, not so much to honor Francis Bacon as to announce an intention to include empirical sciences as an inalienable part of the curriculum. When Bethany College was founded in 1840, Alexander Campbell's positive attitude towards science meant that he included it within the biblical framework he established at the college; his attitudes toward men of science and theirs toward him were highly cordial. It was indeed a doctor of the Bethany circle in whom an exaltation based in part on the rising sciences was to reach its apogee.

The first missionary sent out by the Christian Churches was a physician, J. T. Barclay. He went to Jerusalem, which was chosen as the most biblically appropriate place to start a new missionary enterprise. The evangelistic results were negligible. The literary result was a remarkable volume entitled *The City of the Great King*.[34] The book was divided into three parts: "Jerusalem As It Was," "Jerusalem As It Is," and "Jerusalem As It Is To Be." Each portion reflects the acceptance of a different science. In Dr. Barclay's time archaeology was a very new science, but he realized its significance. In his generation, Dr. Barclay exhibited a passion for archaeological accuracy which is the prototype of the zeal with which J. W. McGarvey in his time measured and counted in the Holy Land every step over which he was able to walk, and of the comprehensive scope with which in our time Dr. Jack Finegan produced his definitive *Light From the Ancient Past* and *The Archaeology of World Religions.* The second section of Dr. Barclay's book was a fine piece of reporting: it is 19th century socio-economic geography of a high order for that period. The third section of the book, "Jerusalem As It Is To Be," is such a piece of literature as it is now most difficult to come by. It is a combination of technocracy and apocalypse, a unique species of Millennialism. Using Jeremiah 31, Ezekiel 45 and Zechariah 14 as literal prophecy, Dr. Barclay envisions what could occur in the Holy Land if indeed at the coming of the Lord "living waters shall flow out from Jerusalem, half of them to the eastern sea, and half of them to the western sea." (Zech. 14:8) Without having to invoke miracle, for great springs sometimes do burst forth naturally, Dr. Barclay points out the natural benefits that such streams would make possible. The steep drop of 5,000 feet to the floor of the Jordan Valley is more than adequate to provide energy to empower extensive industrial enterprises. The eastward stream would fill the basin of the Dead Sea until once again its waters would empty southward into the Gulf of Akbar. With circulation restored the waters of a former Dead Sea would be sweetened and enlivened. The eastward and the westward streams would provide ample irrigation for the lands of Zion, both for Jordania to the east and the Negeb to the southwest. The westward stream would provide navigational access to the Mediterranean Sea, and a railway could certainly also be built. Furthermore, suggests Dr. Barclay, it is not unreasonable to suppose that the waters of such a stream might be so specially endowed with mineral and other properties that the vegetation watered by them, and the livestock fed upon that vegetation would provide a nourishment by which man himself would be enhanced in stamina and stature. A loftier race could appear to inhabit the City of the Great King.

For Walter Scott the glorious future would come about because America had achieved a proper political system. For Dr. Barclay it would come through purely natural means. Face to face with the world, and constantly needing to give practical guidance to his followers, Alexander Campbell was far more cautious and more sophisticated in his assessment of the world. Campbell did believe in the possibility of progress, and he could entertain the idea of a millennial achievement on the face of the earth. He did not disdain science, but for him the millenium could not be accounted for in any such natural terms as the bursting forth of a new spring. Alexander Campbell probed more deeply.

Like his father who saluted America by using the Declaration of Independence as a model for his Christian Declaration, Alexander Campbell saluted his nation upon every annual celebration of the Declaration of Independence by using the day to write a serious address. But Alexander Campbell was not turning to political systems to account for his idea of millennium. For him, science and politics were not redemptive apart from the Christian character of those who employed science or were responsible for government. The millennium would emerge with the increasing Christianization of society, and the agency of that Christianization was the church. For Alexander Campbell the Church of Christ on earth was the Millennial Harbinger, and often enough his advice to his followers was to devote themselves to the work of the church without concern for or involvement in political life.[35]

Like his father before him, Alexander Campbell had a strong aversion to any degree of religious establishment, and most of his political activity can be understood in terms of drawing a clear distinction between church and state. He did not deny that man is a political animal, but he was more concerned that his followers have a distinct recognition of their religious and Christian nature. Therefore he opposed the incorporation of churches. To him it felt like a step toward establishment, and, in any case, for the congregation incorporated it clouded their sense of the distinction between church and state. He was even more opposed to the various kinds of moral societies which were wide-spread upon the American frontier, societies which were against liquor, or slavery, or vices of other sorts. These societies were characterized by a tendency to become vigilante groups, tempted to take the law into their own hands. Even when not so extreme they were constantly seeking to effect legislation enforcing their ideals. For moral and spiritual purposes they were seeking to employ the arm of the state. Aroused to strong terms by such political manouvering, Campbell asserted that by it, "The landmarks between the kingdom of Satan and the Kingdom of God are wholly defaced."[36] Since the church itself is the agent of moral and spiritual reform, the activities of the moral societies verged on an alliance of church and state. Campbell did not usually imply that the state is the kingdom of Satan. His more frequent attitude was that religion is more important than politics, the Church more significant than the State. But the state was not insignificant, and when the Virginia Constitutional Convention was called in 1829 Mr. Campbell won a seat in it. He was a believer in the social compact, and in the convention concerned himself most with the basis of representation, standing against property-based suffrage and affirming that "each man deserves as much voice in the affairs of government as every other." For him the chief ends of government were defending the nations, maintaining order, securing justice and freedom, and though, typical of his time, he entertained no such concept as the welfare state, he did feel that the state bore some responsibility for human welfare, especially in the realm of public education. None the less, in contrast to Scott's enthusiasm, Alexander Campbell tended to despair of political institutions. It was Christianity which would bring the millennium through the millennial church. He certainly did not develop any program of Christian social action, and as late as the 1840s tended to discount the significance of voting. He argued openly against Christians becoming members of political parties on the ground that politics is not where the Christian believer should expend his energies. The place for the Christian is in the work of the church which harbingers the millennium. One cannot but wonder whether he also instinctively resisted political parties because they tended to breed a spirit of factionalism, and that spirit might easily transvert into the spirit of religious sectarianism.

Since his political position was so generally quietist, it is surprising, though none the less typical of Campbell's nature, that when he did become involved in a particular issue he was strongly involved, and typically made his involvement effective. The effectiveness was in large part the result of the clarity of Campbell's thought. When the transportation of mails on Sunday was challenged by a strict sabbatarianism Alexander Campbell was almost a lone ministerial voice raised in defense of the Sunday movement of the mails. Here, as with the moral societies, he recognized that a particular religious doctrine was being forced upon the state. In this instance, it was not only that Campbell's own position was that the Sabbath was made for man and not man for the Sabbath, nor that halting of mail transport on Sunday was detrimental to society. Much more important was the fact that in this case, as with the moral societies, by forcing a particular doctrine upon the State, the clear line between state and Church was in danger.

Perhaps there is no one event in Campbell's life which

indicates the stature of his instinct more than his engagement in debate with the great socialist Robert Owen.[37] Alexander Campbell could tell his people that the thing to do about moral societies was to leave them alone. He could not ignore the challenge to the Christian Church and its ministry involved in Robert Owen's general challenge to debate any representative of the Christian ministry who would come forward. Owen may have been surprised when any one took up the challenge, but he knew that Campbell was a powerful religious force in that Ohio Valley where Robert Owen was seeking to actualize his social ideas in a Rappite colony at New Harmony, Indiana.

The American frontier sensed that something big was going to happen when these two men met in debate. The occasion of it was in Cincinnati, Ohio, April 13-23, 1829, and it drew great audiences. In terms of its effective excitement of a large number of persons the debate was probably the most successful single adult education project of that year in the American nation. It is amazing to think of the intellectual stimulation provided on the frontier by this event. It is the more amazing because the issues of the debate were never engaged by the protagonists. The debate may be little enough read these days, but it was read in its entirety some years ago by Paul Douglas, the present Senator from Illinois. He read it while on the faculty of the University of Chicago, and in the late 1930s accepted an invitation from the students of Disciples Divinity House to talk to them about the debate. His major comment was that Campbell and Owen sailed past each other like ships in the night neither acknowledging the lights of the other.

In his own day, Robert Owen was known as an atheist. If he had been the typical 19th century atheist, Campbell would have been able to engage him at the points of Owen's negations. Actually, Robert Owen was what would today be called a secularist. He was neither for nor against God.

He simply ignored the whole theistic notion. Robert Owen was a new type of man who has become more common in our century. He did not ignore religion. Indeed he accused it of being a demoralizing factor in society. Campbell soon realized that his task was not that of defending the Christian notion of God, but that of combating a man whose whole account of the world used no concepts of divinity at all, and who proposed the possibility of a satisfactory society on the basis of worldly terms alone. In the debate Owen's affirmations consisted of twelve propositions which amount to a sociological determinism. The principles were abstract in type, and rationalistic in mood. Subjoined were Owen's negative propositions. These were that all religions are founded in ignorance, and because they are opposed to unchanging natural laws they are a source of strife, vice and misery. They are a bar to the formation of a society embodying the virtues of intelligence and goodwill. Furthermore, they are maintained only by the tyranny of the unscrupulous clerical few over the ignorant many.

Though Campbell was cultivated enough in Enlightenment and Rationalist thought to have engaged Owen on his own terms, Campbell's instinct led him to argue on other grounds before the great audiences, and for their sake rather than for Robert Owen's. He developed themes based on biblical materials. Whatever the errors of his historicity, what he was doing was to appeal to the concrete realities of a history. He must have deepened in many of his listeners the foundations, not for arguments that would defeat the secularist, but of a faith that would be secure against the secularist's arguments. Owen seems to have run out of steam first; Campbell took the opportunity to fill out the time for the edification of the people. His performance as debater and orator culminated in a twelve-hour speech which occupied several successive sessions of the debate.

Certainly Campbell understood the challenge of what we

today call secularism, especially in so noble and worthy an opponent as Robert Owen. In later years Campbell said that of all his opponents in debate, Robert Owen was certainly the most candid, fair and gentlemanly.

If at times the early Christian Churches felt themselves standing over against the world, the movement would soon be more dependent upon the world than it cared at that time to countenance, and perhaps does not yet want to countenance. In the preceding chapter it was pointed out that in the sixty years between 1832 and 1890, there was a rapid growth not only in the number of Christian Church congregations, but also of all sorts of organizations in which Christian church members bound themselves together for missionary, educational and benevolent purposes. If one asks the question, "Where did these Christian Church members find guidance for the organization of their societies?" the answer, negatively, is that they did not get it from the New Testament. They had already so interpreted their New Testaments that their doctrine of the church could not contain any principles which offered guidance for the establishment and operation of any organizational forms other than those of the local congregations. By some Christian Church members this was taken to mean that the only agency through which Christians might carry out their work was the local congregation. Actually, there is no single community which identifies itself with the original Union of 1832 which has in fact practiced so strict a congregationalism—neither among the Churches of Christ, nor the so-called "Independents," and certainly not among those identified by the term "Disciples of Christ." Both Alexander Campbell and Barton W. Stone in their later years became sensitive to the contradiction involved in a system which avowed so strict a congregationalism and at the same time was developing extensive inter-congregational procedures. Both Campbell and Stone were aware that within this contradiction there could emerge uncontrolled abuses. A strict congregationalist theory provides no guidance for inter-congregational activities or for the activities of "societies." Strict congregationalism has no doctrines which provide guide lines by which to establish constitutional controls beyond the local congregation.

What is remarkable is that for so long a time all the heirs of the Union of 1832 preserved a strict congregationalism as their doctrine of the church. Indeed, the more each of these units developed organization the more likely they were to harden in their assertions that they were congregationalist in polity. By 1849 they should have begun to modify the term somehow—perhaps by some such locution as "congregational-societal" or at a little later date "congregational-conventional," since it was by "conventions" that extra-congregational association was achieved. Some such phraseology, or even the barbarism "congregational-societal-conventional" would at least have had the honesty of indicating that as Christians they were caught up into congregations, societies and conventions. But the human mind, not only among the Christian Churches, but through-out all the communions, seems to have been stubborn about categories of church polity. Until relatively recently eccles-iastical theory has remained bound by the idea that there are only three kinds of polity: congregational, presbyterial and episcopal. Furthermore, the traditional congregational-ist doctrine of the Christian Churches was, in their view, dogmatically related to the New Testament. This has meant that in the twentieth century some have tenaciously clung to biblical proofs of the validity of congregational polity while others assert that biblical proofs of such a doctrine are no longer valid. It can be pointed out that when, in what is known as the liberal wing of the Disciples of Christ, the invalidity of the biblical proof of congregationalist polity was acknowledged, instead of raising the question whether in fact they were still congregationalist, they eagerly seized upon a species of philosophic defense of congregational polity. As a result, a significant moment for a deeply probing questioning of their historic character slipped away. This philosophic defense of congregational polity centers in the emergence among Disciples of Christ of a form of nominalism, bolstered by a long standing usage among the Christian Churches of a concept provided by John Locke, and by a new and strange term which found its way into usage within the movement somewhere about 1910.

The first of these three elements of the new philosophic defense of congregationalism was derived from John Locke. In his *Treatise on Civil Government*, Locke had argued that the only way in which a civil government ought regard religious groups was to consider them "voluntary associations of believers." This concept was widely accepted in the Anglo-Saxon world and in Western Europe, and became the basis of a toleration not only toward religion by the state, but also within the religious sphere. A version of this phraseology stands in Thomas Campbell's *Declaration and Address*. The fourth item which the Christian association of Washington, Pennsylvania declares about itself is:

That this society, by no means considers itself a church . . . nor do the members, as such, consider themselves as standing connected in that relation; nor as at all associated for the peculiar purposes of church associations;—but merely as voluntary advocates for church reformation; and, as possessing the powers common to all individuals who may please to associate in a peaceable and orderly manner, for any lawful purpose: namely, the disposal of their time, counsel and property, as they may see cause.[38]

This declaration is full of terms that descend from Locke through both English and American political theory, and when the members of the Christian Association were moved beyond that stage to becoming a Christian congregation they still thought of themselves, so far as church reformation was concerned, as being its voluntary advocates. The years of their alliance with the Baptists did not slacken this understanding of themselves, for the Baptists were also full of the same Lockean-American terminology. Indeed, so pervasively was the phrase "voluntary association of believers" used amongst the Christian Churches, that by the time your lecturer was a seminary student in the mid-1930s, it was commonly accepted as *the* Disciple doctrine of the church; that is, if Christian Church leaders were asked, "What is the Disciple doctrine of the church?" they would most likely answer, "The church is a voluntary association of believers on Jesus Christ." I shall not forget the day when in a class room of Swift Hall at the University of Chicago, W. E. Garrison said, "The term 'voluntary association of believers' is not a church doctrine of the church; it is a political doctrine of the church. As Christians you have other things to teach about the church." At that time his was a relatively lone voice. The concept of a voluntary association of believers was keeping congregationalist theory alive long after it could claim exclusive biblical support.[39]

This artificial situation by which congregationalist theory was kept alive, was further sustained by the introduction about 1910 of the term "local autonomy," an exotic term imported from twentieth century mid-Europeon sociology and political theory. This term became securely engrafted into the complex with which the Christian Churches were still bolstering the theory of strict congregationalism.

The third element was a species of nominalism. Oddly enough, this element of the defense of congregationalism was supplied primarily by a man who had a profound affection for the whole communion of Christian Churches and who, under circumstances other than those which pertained around him, might well have led his brethren into a deeper understanding of communion. But early in his career, events had almost separated him from that communion, and he had preserved his relationship by finding in a local congregation a citadel within which the doctrine of strict congregationalism was a sure defense. In 1929 E. S. Ames wrote:

> Institutions have the defects of their virtue. They multiply the strengths of people by organizing them into united and orderly action . . . But institutions may overwhelm the individual . . . The institutions may come to enlist all the energies of its members until it is regarded as an end in itself . . . The assumption that churches have an infallible standard of faith, and an equally dependable authority for conduct, tends to make them intolerant of dissent or criticism . . .[40]

Then follows a crucial sentence.

> It would be of assistance toward a better practice if the plural term churches were used instead of the expression *the* Church.

A few sentences later come the words:

> Churches (it is significant that in this context the term churches means local congregations) are free associations of individuals, endeavoring by every means to cultivate the highest forms of life that experience and imagination may devise. They have evolved many types. Such churches tend to propagate themselves throughout the community and the world by the same natural, dynamic impulse with which schools, clans, fraternal orders and commercial enterprises project themselves.[41]

E. S. Ames' intellectual power is evident in that in these

terms he could derive a definition of union and thereby
provide satisfaction to his followers regarding an important
aspect of the traditional Christian Church ideal.

> Probably the most significant and fruitful tendencies
> toward union are to be found in local congregations of
> the free churches, where doctrinal issues are likely to be
> the weakest, and where the natural social impulsion to
> neighborly cooperation are the strongest . . . all congrega-
> tional churches are fast becoming union churches . . .
> the creedal churches have relaxed their insistence upon
> acceptance of the ancient articles of faith.[42]

In such statements, there is a dangerous tendency to define
both church and unity without any reference whatsoever
to Christian substance. Let me add, that these statements
which appear in Ames' definitions of the church are an
aberration within the general character of his religion,
which, in another set of lectures, I have demonstrated as
being both substantively and basically Christian.[43] By
pushing nominalism as far as he did E. S. Ames defended
his territory within Christendom, namely a local congregation, but he did not by what he said about churches provide any identification of himself as Christian.

It was not only for suggestions in the area of doctrine
that the Christian Church members were turning to the
world. At a remarkable pace they were doing it with
respect to the practical life of their religion. In the period
of the rapid development of organization that characterized
the last quarter of the 19th century, they freely borrowed
from the ways of the American business community to order
their missionary, educational and benevolent enterprises.
Not only did the communion as a whole grow in complexity.
Local congregations became more complex internally. The
congregations of American Protestantism in every communion had come to be characterized by a richness of lay

activity which resulted in all sorts of organized groupings within the local congregations: choirs, sunday school classes, women's and men's groups. Inspired either by missionary, benevolent or charitable impulses, congregations developed many kinds of institutionalizations within themselves and auxiliary: boy scout troops, similar organizations for girls, settlement houses or other kinds of community facilities. Before other agencies in society took up adult education strongly, the churches were often the scene of various kinds of courses such as stenography, world affairs, domestic sciences, and so on. What came to be called "the institutionalized church" developed, and with it appeared administrative problems. One of the earliest of these problems was the fracturing of the local congregation into several disparate units, relatively independent of each other. This condition was often the starting point for the development of a curious circumstance in which a church building could become the setting for a series of otherwise barely related activities such as a worshiping group, a Sunday school whose constituency hardly over-lapped the worshiping group, and a mid-week recreational club with even less over-lap with either of the other two activities. While this is an extreme illustration it was obvious that the development of such a circumstance was endemic in many congregations which had not found some way to preserve an internal unity.

By the 1930s a number of pastors had begun to seek solutions to the growing administrative problems of their congregations. Many an instance of success might serve to illustrate what happened, but the work of two men in particular will be presented, especially since each of them by the writing of books exercised a wide influence throughout the communion of Christian Churches. Both men were from Missouri. The earlier of them in print was Clarence E. Lemmon, pastor of the First Christian Church in Columbia, Missouri, with a book entitled *The Art of Church Manage-*

*ment,* 1933.[44] C. E. Lemmon was a man of many gifts who served his brotherhood in many ways. As a pastor he was deeply loved by his people. He was effective in the leadership of a congregation which bore special responsibilities for work with students at a large state university. For many years he wrote a column, "The Book Chat," in *World Call,* and was reputed to be one of the two most widely read Disciple ministers in his generation. (W. E. Garrison was the other.) He served as a President of the International Convention. In administration he was highly gifted, and he was so easy at it that he was rarely thought of as an administrator but always as a pastor. Before entering the ministry C. E. Lemmon had become an accountant. In later years his financial acumen served not only his own congregation but also a number of Boards of Christian Churches, and for many years he served the Protestant ministry at large in his capacity as a Director of the Minister's Life and Casualty Union of Minneapolis.

His book, *The Art of Church Management* appeared in 1933. In the simplest terms, the principles which C. E. Lemmon endorsed in the book were unification of administration and clear divisions of labor. The application of the principle of unity meant that all activity units within the church had to be incorporated into a single structure. The principle of the clear divisions of labor meant, first, that policy making and policy enforcing, i.e. legislative and administrative activities, be strictly differentiated, and that within policy enforcing there be a clear distinction of labors for each of a number of programmatic divisions. These programmatic divisions as listed by C. E. Lemmon included Membership, Worship, Education, Missions, Women's Work, Property, Finance, and "others as desired." The chairmen of these programmatic divisions sat with the minister as an Advisory Council or Cabinet, and constituted the major policy enforcing group. The pastor sat with the

Official Board of Deacons, Elders and Deaconesses which was the policy making body. There might or might not be some other persons beside the pastor who were members of both the policy making and policy enforcing units. The model structure as drawn up by C. E. Lemmon did not make it mandatory that anyone other than the pastor stand in such a link-relationship.

Dr. Lemmon's plan was certainly a major step out of chaos, but in practical usage two short comings have become clear. One is that it was left to the chance of election by the congregation whether anyone in addition to the pastor would stand as a link between policy making and policy enforcing, between legislation and administration. A second short coming is that the list of "Divisions" of labor had not been so carefully rationalized that the multiplication of divisions under the category of "others as desired" could be avoided. Both of these short comings were corrected a decade later in the book entitled *The Church Functioning Effectively* by O. L. Shelton,[45] the minister of Independence Boulevard Christian Church, Kansas City, Missouri, later Dean of the School of Religion of Butler University. Dr. Shelton's writings have probably had the widest effect on local Christian church organization of any single piece of Christian Church literature since Alexander Campbell's *Christian Baptist* essays on "The Restoration of the Ancient Order of Things." What Dr. Lemmon called "administrative divisions," Dr. Shelton called "functions," and it is as "the functional system" that O. L. Shelton's proposals for the government of local congregations is popularly known. Dr. Shelton's list of functions is more tightly reasoned, more finely rationalized, than Dr. Lemmon's list of divisions. Experience has in general confirmed the plan seen in successive stages in these successive books by C. E. Lemmon and O. L. Shelton, though it has also begun to reveal some inadequacies. However, it is not our purpose in these chapters to do the work of a practical theology by deriving a scheme for the political organization of local congregations. What we are concerned to point out is that in this century the Christian Churches have experienced an enormous increase in practical activities and organization and are beginning to recognize that this organizational life of the churches can be discussed in the abstract terms of what, in academic circles, is known as administrative science.

General administrative science is based on the fact that whenever men are in association—for whatever purposes—certain abstract principles are operative. Furthermore, it has come to be realized that these principles are not only operative in the life of a congregation, they are also operative in the life of any kind of religious association, independent or cooperative, Church of Christ or Disciple of Christ.

General administrative science is by no means the only science from which the churches were deriving insights about the nature of the church. In the city of Chicago, at the close of the First World War, a Disciple of Christ seminary student became the pastor of the Douglas Blvd. Christian Church. Almost immediately, the church began to perish, but when it died the young minister, S. C. Kincheloe, was sure that he had not killed it. On the contrary he was sensitive to the changes in the immediate community which were factors in the dissolution of that congregation. Dr. Kincheloe moved on from insights about this one congregation to the principle that congregations are, in some regard, a function of their communities. Through a lifetime, S. C. Kincheloe explored the relationship between congregations and their social environments, and became the originator of an American sociology of religion centering on the ecological factors in church life. The value of Dr. Kincheloe's work was soon sensed throughout American Protestantism. Councils and Federations of churches developed Bureaus for Sociological Research and Survey, as did many communions. Sociology of Religion has expanded into the critical re-examination of the kinds of structures by which Christian community shall be maintained in a neighborhood.

The history of a church in Chicago illustrates both the significance of the rise of a sociology of religion, and the dilemmas inherent in congregationalist doctrine. About a century ago, a congregation of Christians formed the Jackson Blvd. Christian Church in a new section of the city. The church flourished. A large sanctuary was built, and later an adjoining educational and recreational building was added. After a glorious half-century, the neighborhood began to decay. The congregation lost both membership and financial strength. A secular organization leased the educational building to house community services. The congregation originally entered into this relationship because they thought it might have evangelistic value. It did not. For many years, two distinct organizations used the buildings without becoming spiritually integrated. Then the sanctuary burned down. The congregation realized that it could survive only if it repossessed the educational building for its own use. That, it could not financially afford to do. Furthermore, the community was by now passing through the ultimate stages of a fully bull-dozed transition from a white neighborhood of single dwellings to a colored neighborhood of high-rise apartments. Suddenly, the question of the existence in that place of a congregation of the Christian churches could no longer be made by the congregation itself. It had become predominantly transient. In this vacuum of decision, power was exercised by the Chicago Disciples Union, a city missionary society. The Union was encumbered with financial obligations relative to the location of new congregations. The sites of these new congregations had been determined with the assistance of sociological surveys. Similar surveys were now used to help decide whether a Christian service could be carried on in the neighborhood of the Jackson Blvd. building if a small congregation could be maintained. An affirmative decision was reached. However, the congregation could be maintained only if subsidized. At the time, the Chicago Disciples Union did not have resources for a subsidy. The Union referred the matter to the Illinois Christian Missionary Society, a state organization, which also, at that time, had no funds available for subsidy. An appeal was next made to the United Christian Missionary Society, a national organization. The appeal was not made by the congregation, but by the city Union. In other words, the fate of a local congregation was now being decided by the initiative of a city association in cooperation with a state and a national agency. The national agency was able to provide the subsidy, and decided to do so after it carried out certain sociological surveys. Interestingly enough, the possibility of close cooperation with a Roman Catholic setlement house in the neighborhood was a factor influencing the national agency to provide support for the congregation at Jackson Blvd. Christian Church.

From a strictly "congregationalist" point of view, the procedures recounted about the Jackson Blvd. church are very "unorthodox." The principles by which a witness has been kept in the Jackson Blvd. buildings ignore most of the principles of historical congregationalism. At the Roman Catholic settlement house the driving force is a Roman Catholic sister whose piety is enlightened by a grasp of sociological principles which would delight S. C. Kincheloe.

It is not only the sociological sciences that the Christian churches have used to gain practical understanding of Christian community and life. Twenty years before S. C. Kincheloe began his work, E. S. Ames had carried out studies in the psychology of religious communities, and his book, *The Psychology of Religious Experience* (1910)[46] established his world reputation as a scholar of the religious life. Ames' studies were important in helping the churches further the evangelical significance of religious education.

During the 1920s, the principles whereby general educational theory could be brought to the enhancement of religious education were provided to the major communions of America by W. C. Bower, a Disciple of Christ. More recent aspects of psychology have been incorporated into the movement of the Christian churches through the work of Dr. Charles Kemp in Fort Worth, Dr. Jack Shirley of Lexington, Kentucky, Dr. Harmon Bro of Chicago, and Dr. Marcus Bryant of Des Moines, Iowa. Seminary education now typically includes instruction in pastoral counseling and care based on the sciences of man.

And what shall be said about the establishment of the Disciples of Christ Historical Society in 1941 except that it was a logical step in the process whereby the Christian Churches were laying hold of that most basic of all the social sciences, namely, history.

In this twentieth century, the Christian Churches have incorporated into their thinking a vast amount of scientific understanding intimately related to their conception of the church and vitally related to their actual church practice. Is this scientific material extraneous to the traditional Christian Church concept of the church? In terms of the strict understandings of the origins, yes. But in terms of what happened shortly thereafter something else must be said.

Despite their original assertions that they would accept only the Bible as the Divine Standard, the members of the Christian Church movement early found that they simply could not answer all the questions of ecclesiastical practice by reference to the New Testament. They found themselves acting beyond explicit New Testament guidance. When challenged for the reasons behind their actions they said it was "expedient" so to do. Presently they had elevated "expediency" into a principle. It stands among the principles in Alexander Campbell's *Christian System,* and it served the churches well in freeing them from what might have been a most rigid application of the idea of a blueprint of church order in the New Testament. So far as I know, the doctrine of expediency has never been basically repudiated by any section of the movements stemming from the work of Stone and the Campbells. But the principle of expediency has presented difficulties. It can be the justification for highly personalized and individualized actions. What some members of the Christian Churches have recognized is that by scientific inquiry an area of expediency which might otherwise be chaotic may be rationalized, ordered, and reduced to firm principles which all can acknowledge, not in any final dogmatic way, but in practical terms which enlighten cooperative activities. Such principles would always be held subject to re-examination as their limitations begin to come into view.

It is certainly clear by now that among the churches stemming from the Union of 1832 many an element of the world has entered in. More recently these elements have come to be recognized for what they are. There is no longer any strict avoidance of the inventions of men. There is a growing recognition that it is impossible for the church to exist, or for the gospel to be preached, without any mixture of philosophy, the traditions of men, or the rudiments of the world. In this regard, the Christian Churches are today passing through an interesting crisis of conscience. For some decades, their membership has been aware that their practice has included much that derives from human sources other than the New Testament. Much of that membership has felt that this condition is a falling away from an earlier pristine state in which our forefathers did succeed in fashioning Christian congregations free of any mixture of philosophy, vain decit, the traditions of men and the rudiments of the world, and without inculcating anything of human authority, or private opinion or inventions of men. What is now coming to consciousness is that such a pristine condition never did exist, nor was it ever achieved by our forefathers even though they thought they had done so. What is now being more fully recognized is that the nature of the church is such that it never exists except with the involvement of as much humanity as divinity in its character. It is time that the descendants of the Campbells and Stone asked themselves the question, "Can the organization that is the Body of Christ be anything other than a divine-human organization?"

Is it not possible that the traditional Christian Church doctrine of a Christianity devoid of human inventions is similar to the docetic heresy of an earlier time which saw Christ only as divine and failed to acknowledge the true and full humanity that is just as much part of the nature of Christ as his divinity.

To emphasize this point let us in this inaugural lectureship of the Reed Lectures turn to the inaugural lectures of another Lectureship established within the communion of Christian Churches. I read part of a paragraph from a chapter in *Prospecting for a United Church* by Angus Dun, then the Episcopal Bishop of Washington, D. C.

The place of worship (of a congregation) is the home or temple of God's people in their character as his people. It is also his house, his temple. He owns it; he dwells there. "The Lord is in his holy temple." So his people gather there to meet him. The book that is read there is the book of his people; the words spoken there are men's words, but the book and the words are likewise his or shared with him. The most distinctive actions, the sacraments or ordinances performed there are acts of his people; they are also in some sense God's acts, or acts with reference to him. The minister or the priest is certainly a man, in a special sense the church's man, but he is likewise God's minister, God's priest. Even Christ, supremely Christ, as the central and originative meeting point of God and his people, partakes of this duality. He is God's Christ and man's Christ, God's and man's, God and Man.[47]

This moving passage might well be the conclusion of this lecture if it did not point us on to one more consideration. As members of the Christian Churches have come to recognize that the church cannot be validly understood apart from its human  nature, as well as in terms of its divine nature, they have come to recognize that the church in its essence cannot be understood apart from the concept of development. This means that they have begun to move on from a classical style of thought regarding the church to an historical style of thinking. A classical style of thought about the church is one which presupposes that in its formal character the earthly church is unchanging. From that point of view, only those forms of organization are properly called church which conform to the classical pattern. All variations therefrom are wrong. The historic style of thought about the church recognizes that in its formal character, whatever the continuities that keep the church true to its Lord, the church is developmental. This historical style of thought knows that if the church is true to its Lord, the church will suffer development. Failure on the part of the church to develop in accordance with new historical situations would be failure to be the church, failure to be true to the Lord. There is here no question of the church adjusting to the world. The problem for the church is to adjust to itself, for it is only the church when it is doing the work of the Lord; unless the church keeps adjusting itself to whatever is the work of the Lord in each new day, the church is not adjusting to itself, but remaining conformed to the world's decay, and thereby becoming obsolete.

In the last paragraph, the terms "classical thinking" and "historical thinking" were used. I heard these terms used at Vatican Council II by John Courtney Murray, S. J. He used them to designate a shift in the style of Roman Catholic thought regarding the nature of the church. These terms are similarly useful to designate a shift in the style of Christian Church thought about the nature of the church. The fact that these terms can serve to describe what is happening doctrinally in both Catholic and Protestant thought indicates that dialogue with Rome is indeed under way. With that dialogue the next chapter deals.

# III

## *Dialogue with Rome*

When the Union of 1832 took place, the proportion of Roman Catholics in the American population was very small. At that time, and since, they have had their greatest density in areas other than those in which the Christian Churches have had their greatest density. Much of the time, the Roman Catholic and the Christian Churches have hardly been within hailing distance of each other, much less on speaking terms. In this regard, however, the Christian Churches have been similar to most of the rest of Protestantism which has shared the depth of separation which has characterized the two great sections of Christendom known as Roman Catholicism and Protestantism.

It is valid to raise here the question of the relationship of Roman Catholicism to the Disciple discovery of the church. The question can be answered because upon two very important historic occasions, members of the Christian Churches were the spokesmen, not only for their own communions but for American Protestantism generally in relationship to Rome. Furthermore it is an important matter because it is evident that a very different future with respect to Catholic-Protestant relationships is in the making, and Disciples of Christ have a place in that future. It is a significant historical fact that the Christian Churches have their clearest instance of progress from debate through discussion to dialogue in their relationship to Roman Catholicism.

Both Thomas and Alexander Campbell brought to

America a strong prejudice against Roman Catholicism. Their attitude was not only typical of the attitude in the British Isles and in Ireland where Catholic-Protestant tension was high. Their attitude contained also, through the Hugenot heritage of Mrs. Thomas Campbell, a dimension from the Continent and the memories of St. Bartholomew's Eve. Nonetheless, during years of great turbulence in Ireland from 1795 to 1805, Thomas Campbell was never swept off his feet into violence of attitude, much less of act. In so far as he had to be involved in the political turmoil that swept around him, he held his involvement to the well-tempered levels of reason and persuasion. It was not always easy to do, and perhaps the first paragraphs of a discussion of Christian Church and Catholic relationships ought to begin with more than this brief comment on Thomas Campbell's involvement prior to coming to America. The story is available elsewhere, however.[48]

The removal to Western Pennsylvania did carry the Campbells into a part of the world in which Roman Catholics were so few in number that their presence did not arouse against them the kinds of feelings that had often been stirred in Ireland. In the *Declaration and Address* the Roman church is mentioned only obliquely when Campbell lists among the blessings of America its lack of connection to those "nations that have given their strength and power unto the beast." In these nations, said Campbell, "of course no adequate reformation can occur until the word of God is fulfilled, and the vials of his wrath poured out upon them."[49] But by the time he wrote those words, Thomas Campbell had come to America and would never again be personally involved at close range with the Roman Catholic Church. Alexander Campbell in 1809, did not expect any close involvement with the Roman Church, and it did not come for more than twenty-five years. In the meantime the Church of Rome did provide the iconoclastic Alexander with an armament of terms, and attitudes, a vocabularly and a stance, with which he argued against "Protestant popery"—namely Presbyterianism. Especially in his anti-clerical years he was arguing against "the Clergy and their Kingdom," using against established and right-wing Protestant groups many of the same arguments which these groups themselves had used against Rome.[50] Campbell's attitude during his early *Christian Baptist* years was that whenever the clergy were set up in distinction to the laity (thereby possessing a special sacramental preserve) the conditions were set for an inevitable progress toward a clerical reign involving the accumulation of economic power. This accumulation worked in favor of an establishment which would be given theoretical justification even if it could not be given practical effect in political power—which was the ultimate objective. The Roman Catholic Church was the extreme instance of this trend, but by no means the one closest at hand. Alexander Campbell feared the little Protestant popes just as much as he feared the Pope of Rome who was but the model of the ultimate intention of all clericalism. We must not forget that throughout the life-time of both the Campbells, the Pope of Rome was also the sovereign and absolute temporal ruler of an earthly kingdom, the Papal States. This kingdom straddled the Italian Peninsula as the most tenacious, if not the most formidable, barrier to a United Italy. The Campbells undoubtedly were sympathetic though far from involved in the rising effort of Italian nationalism to effect a united Italy.

If in the later 20th century we must remind ourselves about the temporal nature of this Papacy in 1809, we must also remind ourselves about the character of the establishment which characterized Protestantism at that time—a kind of establishment in contrast to which any establishment now left in Christendom is a pale shadow. In 1809, the system of Protestant denominationalism was relatively new, and was only just beginning to replace the system of Protestant territorialism. The first amendment to the Constitution was indeed an American experiment. In the rest of the Protestant world the practice that still prevailed generally was that the religion of the ruler had to be the religion of the land, which meant that Protestants visited upon each other as well as upon Catholics, civil and political disabilities which at times broke out into cruel persecutions. Nor should it be forgotten in assessing Campbell's attitude towards Presbyterians that of all the American colonies, now become states, the one which was responding most slowly to the implications of the First Amendment was Massachusetts in which the dominant group was Presbyterian. In 1809 it could still with reason be asked whether or not American Presbyterianism had fully rejected the notion of establishment or whether it harbored within itself clerical attitudes which still implied establishment as their goal.

In the eyes of the greater number of American Christians the new denominational system seemed like a very good thing. W. E. Garrison has written:

Both the concept of the church and the actuality of the church in history must be taken into account. The church was a very complicated item in their Christian heritage. Nearly everyone admitted, if the point were urged, that the church was, in some sense, a unity. Actually, of course it was divided into many parts. In the time of our founding fathers most American Christians had come to believe that this divided condition was a very good arrangement. The denominational system was in fact much more decent and humane than the programs of persecution for the enforcement of a unity of uniformity which had preceded it. Our fathers inherited not only the church, . . . but also the denominational system as, in the common view, the most satisfactory form—or even the only form—under which the church could exist under American conditions. We know, of course, what they thought of that.[51]

"What they thought of that" was based not alone on its failure to express Christian unity. In so far as longing for establishment lurked within denominationalism it held the seeds for a return to the past—and for that matter still does. Throughout the period of the *Christian Baptist*, Alexander Campbell paid little attention to the Roman Catholic Church as he strove ardently against the more immediate threat of Presbyterian clericalism. But the course of American history was changing as a new tide of immigration swelled in the 1820s and 1830s. This new tide included a a high proportion of Roman Catholics. The Scotch-Irish Protestants of an earlier immigrant flow now found themselves followed by the same Irish Catholics they had left behind. These new immigrants poured into the cities of the Eastern sea-board. Whereas the earlier waves of migration had settled the land, this new wave was absorbed largely into those centers of the American Northeast where a developing industrial belt was just beginning to need an enormous labor supply. Presently the nation was agitated by fears that this new wave of immigration represented a subversion of the political ways worked out by the young American nation. These fears prompted the development among those descended from the earlier settlers of an attitude known as "nativism" which at times became extremely emotional and uncritical and rabidly anti-Catholic. Alexander Campbell did not join this "nativist" wave in America any more than had his father joined either the Society of the Orangemen or even the Society of the United Irishmen back in Ireland. But by the 1830's he began to pay some attention in the *Millennial Harbinger* to the increase in the Catholic proportion of the population, particularly because he believed they were dominated by the

Jesuits. Even from the start, Alexander Campbell felt that the true ark against the immigrant flood was not nativist attack but education, and it was undoubtedly with educational intention that Campbell entered upon debate with Bishop Purcell of Cincinnati. In January, 1837, Campbell was back in the Queen City of the Ohio Valley, and though the debate lacked the extent of popular excitement that surrounded the earlier debate with Robert Owen, it was to prove another instance of good adult education.

The Campbell-Purcell debate is interesting reading at any time,[52] and especially worth while reading in this new ecumenical age. The Catholic bishop, whatever his powers of polemic may have been, was not a skilled debater. His opponent was a skilled debater. Actually Bishop Purcell was not much of a polemicist, and in later years Campbell was to say that for candor, fairness and gentlemanliness, of all his debate opponents Purcell was second only to Robert Owen. This estimate is the more remarkable when one reads the topics of the debate, for Campbell certainly said some very harsh things about the Roman Catholic Church. Campbell, as was usually the case, had the stronger hand in defining the topics for debate. Topic number four was "The Roman Catholic Church is the 'Babylon' of John, the 'Man of Sin' of Paul, and the empire of the 'Youngest Horn' of Daniel's Sea Monster." These are not exactly nice epithets, but Bishop Purcell endured them with good grace and urbanity.

Throughout the debate Campbell sought to be representative of Protestantism. In the three debates which have concerned us, Campbell has been a different champion in each debate. Against Owen in 1829 he propounded the claims of Christianity, indeed of the religious point of view. Against Purcell in 1837 he propounded the claims of Protestantism. Against Rice in 1843 he propounded the claims of the Christian Churches against Presbyterianism.

Of these three debates it was when he sought to be the advocate of Protestantism against Purcell that he was at the greatest disadvantage, and his opponent knew the disadvantage in which Campbell stood. Protestantism is not unified doctrinally, and time after time Purcell caught Campbell up. When Campbell argued against apostolic succession Purcell caught him by quotation from other Protestants. When Campbell quoted a sharp criticism of the episcopal and papal systems from Edward Gibbon's *Decline and Fall of the Roman Empire,* Purcell closed in on his opponent with a devastating rebuttal.[53] Purcell pointed out that Gibbon was born into a Protestant family. As a young man Gibbon had become acquainted with the Catholic Church, and finally had decided that he wanted to join that church. His parents had rabidly opposed this move, and Gibbon found stability at last in the rejection and hatred of all forms of Christianity. This hatred, Purcell pointed out, had a root not in Catholic intolerance but in Protestant intolerance. A fair estimate of Bishop Purcell is that he was the most widely read and cultivated of all of Campbell's opponents.

From the standpoint of our concern with the discovery of the church and the doctrine of the church, the first two points of the debate are the most important. The first topic was: "The Roman Catholic institution, sometimes called the 'Holy Catholic, Apostolic Church' is not now, nor was she ever, catholic, apostolic or holy; but is a sect in the fair import of that word, older than any other sect now existing, not the 'Mother and Mistress of all Churches' but an apostasy from the only true, holy, apostolic and catholic church of Christ."

The first thing to be noticed about this topic is that it committed Alexander Campbell to the definition of the true church in terms of the classical tradition that the church of Christ has the marks of unity, holiness, apostolicity and catholicity. It was not typical of Campbell's followers in his own day, nor was it to be for many decades that they would define the church in these classical categories. Campbell had already taught his followers to define the church by the term "New Testament" and by that term to mean formal order. He had rarely led them in seeking for meanings in the understanding of the church as One, Holy, Catholic and Apostolic. Furthermore, the fact that these terms had been caught up into the creeds tended to put something of a curse on them from the Disciple point of view. Only in recent years has this set of terms again appealed to some Disciples as an outline for significant discussion of the nature of the church. It is significant to realize that these categories were unreservedly accepted by Alexander Campbell. He did not argue against this phraseology as being unscriptural but asserted that the Roman Catholic institution did not in practice match this definition.

A second point to notice about the first topic of the debate is that it drew from Campbell a statement that he advocated order in the Church.[54] From the outset Campbell understood that his quarrel with Catholicism was not a quarrel against order on behalf of some spiritistic or pietist enthusiasm or experimentalism, or on behalf of that kind of anti-nomian idea of "liberty" which sets freedom over against order. Campbell knew that without order there is no possibility of freedom but only the inevitability of chaos in which all freedom is lost in the face of arbitrary and uncontrolled powers. Therefore on the occasion of this debate, however much at other times he may have veered toward anti-nomianism, he girded himself with the concept of order, declaring, "I am the advocate of order, of Christian ministry, of deacons and bishops in the church. Without order no society can exist, and therefore no reasonable man can object either to order or authority in the church." Campbell's argument against Roman Catholicism was that its order is not scriptural, and therefore is the wrong order.

There are a number of passages in Campbell's development of the first point of debate which have an unexpected relationship to the conversations at present developing in the Commission on Brotherhood Restructure. During the meeting of the Commission in Chicago, June 21 to 24, 1965, one of the committees brought in a report in which it used the phrase "order of the ministry." This phrase met with considerable resistance and occasioned much discussion. The usual argument against the phrase was that it suggested a distinction between the clergy and the laity, and furthermore, the term "order" suggested a lack of freedom. In terms of historical points of view, these arguments are obviously current versions of anti-clericalism in the first instance, and of anti-nomianism in the second instance. In the sessions of the Commisssion, those who were appealing to Campbell as an advocate of ministerial order referred only to his better known *Christian System*. The lesser known Campbell-Purcell debate would have served their purposes the more, especially since here Campbell does not make the mistake of countering what he considers a wrong order by arguments which would dissolve the concept of order, but by countering in the name of what he considers Christian order.

Campbell's chief argument against the order of the Roman Catholic institution was levelled at the papacy, and particularly at the notion of papal infallibility. In this connection is it Purcell's attitude which will most interest us. Just as in the matter of order Campbell did not dissolve the term, so regarding infallibility, Purcell did not dissolve the relationship of this term to the papacy. He acknowledged that in some regard the Pope is infallible, but Purcell insisted that the nature of the infallibility must be carefully understood. It is important to realize that this debate was taking place more than thirty years before the first Vatican

Council and there was as yet no dogmatic decree regarding papal infallibility. When that decree was passed it was, of course, not in terms of the wild extremisms of Archbishop Manning and the more fanatical papalists, but was in the restricted terms of an infallibility which pertains when the Pope is speaking ex cathedra, i.e. officially, in the area of faith or morals. Throughout the debate, though he accepted the category of papal infallibility, Bishop Purcell did argue in terms of the minimal meaning. Campbell constantly counter-attacked by asserting that the idea of infallibility could mean only a general and total absolutism. Since Purcell found that his theory of infallibility would not disuade Campbell from this extremist theory, the Bishop shifted his argument to the ground of practice, presenting actual procedures of the Roman Catholic Church. As an instance, Purcell pointed to the procedures for the election of a bishop. He said, "The pope is not a tyrant . . . I do not derive all my authority from the Pope. The bishops of the United States consult together. They propose candidates . . . three names are sent (with an order of preference indicated) . . . The Pope generally trusts their wisdom and acquiesces in their choice."[55] Now, in this short statement Purcell had not only indicated the untyrranical practice of the Pope; he had asserted that he did not derive all his authority from the papacy. The Campbell-Purcell debate constitutes an interesting prelude to the most important issues of both the First and Second Vatican Councils. In the great decree on *The Nature of the Church* passed by the Second Vatican Council, the Council together with the Pope did indeed decree, as Purcell had indicated, that the bishops do not derive all their power from the Pope, but receive it from their very character as bishops, though they never have this power apart from the Pope. It is indeed exciting to think of a debate in Cincinnati in 1837 rehearsing the great issues of the two Vatican Councils, and it is a mark of the stature of both Purcell and Campbell that it could have been so.

In the second topic of the debate, Campbell argues specifically against the apostolic claims of the Roman Catholic institution particularly as she makes them in terms of apostolic succession. The wording of the topic is that "Her notion of apostolic succession is without any foundation in the Bible, reason or fact; an imposition of the most injurious consequences built on unscriptural and anti-scriptural traditions." Campbell could not in this instance claim the support of the whole of Protestantism, and Purcell, who obviously cherished this concept, quickly pointed to both Episcopalianism and The German Reformed Church as instances of Protestant Churches claiming apostolic succession which indeed the Roman Catholic Church did acknowledge as valid succession. Campbell's argument against the idea of such succession on the basis of historic fact and of reason were acute, but with respect to its relation to Biblical facts Campbell came dangerously close to wiping out the very notion of apostolicity as a mark of the church which in earlier stages of the debate he had upheld. Campbell argued that the apostles can have no successors. It is true, he said, that Christ did empower the apostles who then set up bishops and deacons and the New Testament order. It is these, said Campbell, and not the apostles who have successors. This is a strange turn of argument for it immediately gives the ministry of the church, the bishops and the deacons, a distinction not shared by the rest of the church's membership. This is perhaps the weakest proposal in Campbell's argument. It is in form very similar to the Campbellite doctrine of the Holy Spirit expounded in the *Christian Baptist* and again in the fifth proposition of the debate with Rice. We shall return to this matter later.

In the third topic of the Purcell debate, Campbell argues against the unity of the Catholic church by insisting that she is not uniform in faith and united in her members, but mutable and fallible as any other sect of philosophy or religion, a confederation of sects under a politico-ecclesiastical head. This statement of the case is certainly correct in so far as it does not interpret the Roman Catholic Church as a great monolith, uniform in its faith and practice. It is certainly in this latter way that the vast majority of Protestants have understood Roman Catholicism virtually until this decade of the Second Vatican Council.

When it came to that fourth topic in which Campbell equated the Roman church with "Babylon," the 'Man of Sin' and the "empire of the Youngest Horn of Daniel's Sea Monster," Campbell said much over which we had perhaps best draw the veil. It was under this topic that he elaborated the reasons why the Roman Church could not claim holiness. She is a sect, said Campbell, but her gates are wide as the human race. Since she admits everyone she cannot really claim holiness. "It is all church and no world with her" he continued, and added, "The lusts of the flesh, the lusts of the eyes, and the pride of life are found in her communion." In this argument Campbell came as close as he ever did to defining the true church in pietistic and moralistic terms as a holiness sect, and it is indeed remarkable, knowing as much about Protestantism and his own brethren as he did by the age of forty-nine, that he could not have known how subject he could be to the rebuke, "Let him who is without sin cast the first stone," if Purcell had cared to make it. Purcell did not.

In the fifth topic Campbell declared that Rome's teachings regarding purgatory, auricular confession, indulgences, transubstantiation, supererrogation, etc. are essential to her system, and that they are immoral in their tendency and injurious to the well being of society. The argument proceeded laboriously in ways that need not now delay us. Purcell probably made little impression on either Campbell

or the Protestant portion of the audience in his assertions
that the doctrines mentioned except for transubstantiation
are not essential teachings, but are church interpretations
of the gospel and therefore subject to speculation and modi-
fication.

The sixth and seventh topics have somewhat more immediate interest for Disciples of Christ and their doctrine
of the church. In the sixth proposition Campbell argued
that not withstanding her pretensions to have given us the
Bible, "we are independent of the Roman Church for that
book and its evidence of a divine original." Like most early
nineteenth century Protestants the Campbell-Stone movements thought of the Protestant position in general as an
appeal to the Bible as ultimate authority. Campbell was a
biblical scholar and was well aware of the history of the
formation of the New Testament canon. He was also aware
of the critical problems of authorship and audience that
should be recognized in seeking an understanding of the
Bible. While Campbell was certainly an exponent of textual
or lower criticism, he did still accept the concept of apostolic
authorship of the separate books. He could account for the
process of canonization as being a response on the part of
the early church of the first several centuries to the apostolic authorship. What Campbell did not know, nor did any
Protestants or Catholics in the early 19th. century, was
that the early church as a whole undoubtedly had a place
not only in the collection of the "apostolic writings" but
also in their very formulation. We now understand that the
New Testament writings were dependent not upon the concepts of single authors, even when they had single authors,
but upon the concepts by which preachers and teachers
and ordinary laymen of the early church expressed their
Christian faith. The understanding that the New Testament
books were formed within the matrix of the Christian
community belongs one hundred years after Campbell. At

the present time Protestant and Catholic scholars admit
that together they confront a series of difficult questions
regarding the original relationships between the teachings,
tradition, life and practice of the early Christian community,
the Revelation of God's Word, and the biblical literature
both as single books and as a canonical literature. There is
even in our day still difference of opinion regarding the
limits of the canon. Every Christian acknowledges an
authority to the Bible. But the authorities acknowledged
vary, and constitute in our day a most exciting challenge.
Fortunately it is in this area that Protestant, Catholic and
Jewish scholarship in a new ecumenical age have progressed
farthest. Indeed, it is because for a quarter century such
cooperative scholarship has already been going on that it
was possible for Pope John XXIII to open the latest stage of
the ecumenical movement in 1960 by the establishment of
a wide spread dialogue between Catholics and Protestants.
What Purcell and Campbell said about the Bible in 1837
is outdated, but what their successors on both sides have
subsequently said has already borne great fruit within the
Christian community and is indeed the promise of greater
things to come.

The final point of the Campbell-Purcell debate dealt
with the matters that most stirred the feelings of the nativists. The topic was stated thus: "The Roman Catholic
religion if infallible and unsusceptible of reformation as
alleged is essentially unAmerican, being opposed to the
genius of all free institutions and positively subversive of
them, opposing the general reading of the Scriptures and
the diffusion of useful knowledge among the whole community, so essential to liberty and the permanency of good
government." Lying behind the accusation that Roman
Catholicism was unAmerican was the belief that Catholic
faith meant that all Catholics were committed to the Pope
not only as their spiritual head but as their temporal head,

and that they must inevitably follow the political teachings of their priests, these teachings in turn being dictated from Rome in terms of the Pope's temporal ambition. In 1837 the existence of the Papal States lent great credence to this argument. This idea was further fortified by the behavior of the new immigrant groups. Today we know that these Catholic immigrants, who were the first great wave of immigration into the young nation, behaved in a manner typical of all immigrant groups. But the native Americans of the young nation did not understand that the clustering of these new immigrants into enclaves was not because they wanted to maintain a tight bond of allegiance to a foreign power, but because they needed each other's moral support as they faced the difficulties of finding their place inside an already established society. This was indeed a different problem from the one faced by the nativists' ancestors whose problem had been that of sweeping across an open and empty frontier to establish a society. The colonies had had some experience with cultural enclaves, (for instance the Germans in southern Pennsylvania), but these were negligible episodes in the wilderness. Now there began to come groups which eventually included more Germans, Irish, Scandinavians, Czechs, Italians, Poles, Ukranians and Greeks. What we know now is that these enclaves normally persist for about three generations, by which time the descendants of the immigrants have won their place in American society, and if they continue to cherish some other national heritage it is to add a touch of spice to life, not to subvert America. But when Roman Catholicism began to establish its parochial schools, and when Irish ways and political power became frequent in the American scene, the early nineteenth century could not see the developmental process which we, looking back, can see. There has been a cultural and academic lag in the Roman Catholic community. That gap is closing. There was an economic and therefore a socio-cultural gap between much of the Catholic community and the rest of America. That gap is closing. The Pope is no longer a temporal ruler except for the few acres of Vatican City which can have no imperialistic pretensions, and after ninety-five years experience of freedom from the responsibilities of a temporal sovereign the papacy is currently defined without such responsibilities, and the vast membership of the Catholic Church does not want to see the return of such responsibilities to the papacy. I believe that Catholics would never support such a move, though they would jump to the defense of the physical and personal safety of the Pope and the papal curia—just as Protestants during the Second World War and subsequently sought to succor Christians who suffered under Hitler or who suffer now behind the Iron Curtain.

No matter who won the debate, it must be recognized that in the age in which it was held, the debate was rather an ecumenical than a polemical event, and certainly the twentieth century does not yet show any more sincere expression of the ecumenical spirit than these words:

I disclaim all unkind feelings toward Mr. Campbell or any of his friends, and acknowledge my gratitude to him for enabling me to place my religion in its proper light before the public. I also beg leave respectfully to tender to this audience my thanks for the dignity of their deportment during this debate. Instead of quarreling about religion we ought to be engaged in our vocation of love and peace, as its faithful ministers, and sincere professors. We have all a great deal of work to do to improve the morals of the age, to elevate the standard of literature, to promote by such means as all Christians approve the welfare of our common country . . . These are legitimate pursuits, alike pleasing to God, and useful to man. The world is large enough for us all. Some can in the Abraham and Lot way of settling their difficulties, feed their flocks in one field and some in another; and, as Joseph said to his brethren going home to their father from Egypt, as we are going to one heavenly Father, "see that ye fall not out by the way."[56]

As for Alexander Campbell, after the debate with Bishop Purcell, he was involved in no further controversy or encounter with Roman Catholics except as he did devote himself to the cause of education which, we have remarked, he looked upon as the best way by which all the elements of the American nation would become capable of contributing to the welfare of their common country.

The last topic of the Campbell-Purcell debate, dealing with the relation of Catholicism to the American way, serves as an introduction to the second moment in history when a Disciple of Christ played an important role in Catholic-Protestant relations. The year was 1928. There was then a political situation which stirred up all the issues that were involved in the last topic of the debate a century earlier, for the Democratic Patry nominated as its candidate for the presidency of the United States of America the Governor of the State of New York, the Honorable Alfred E. Smith, a devout Roman Catholic. The nation was swept by the question, "Can a loyal American vote for a Roman Catholic for the National presidency?"

There was need of authoritative discussion of the question from the Protestant point of view. It appeared in a book entitled *Catholicism and the American Mind* by W. E. Garrison,[57] a Disciple of Christ, member of a family highly respected among the Christsian Churches, and, as literary editor of *The Christian Century* acknowledged in Protestantism generally as a great authority on American religious life.

*Catholicism and the American Mind* is an historically

accurate book free of prejudice. It displays a remarkable acquaintance with the Catholicism of the 1920s both in America and elsewhere in the world. W. E. Garrison had traveled widely and well in Europe and had sought to acquaint himself not only with Catholic doctrine and polity, but also with Catholic piety upon which he exercised a critical discrimination. With respect to the latter Dr. Garrison wrote that he had visited such famous shrines as Guadalupe, Einsiedeln and Lourdes, the last, though not the others, appreciatively. Dr. Garrison's profound acquaintance with Catholicism was not typical of his time, and he knew that there was far more involved in understanding Vatican Council I than some simple interpretation of the doctrine of papal infallibility. That dogma, which had been decreed in 1870, had tended to harden Protestant attitudes toward Catholicism as a monolithic structure slipping back into medievalism. Dr. Garrison agreed that it was valid in 1928 to state that Catholic doctrine was slipping back into medievalism, but he carefully kept this issue separated from political matters inherent in the candidacy of Mr. Smith for the presidency. Most Protestants had jumped to the conclusion that the "monolithic" church would never again call a Council. Dr. Garrison probably shared that view, though he was aware that within Catholicism there existed a wide-spread, if inconspicuous, concern regarding the relationships within the church between the papacy, the episcopacy, the priesthood and the laity. Because of his understanding of this issue, *Catholicism and the American Mind* can still be read as a fair introduction to the main issues which were dealt with in Vatican Council II.

For the sensitive reader, therefore, Dr. Garrison provided a volume which corrected many false notions regarding details of Catholicism, and, in its later sections, turned to the great question of the fitness of a Catholic for the presidency. The heart of the problem was whether or not a Catholic was, in the end, temporally subject to a foreign power. In 1928 the Pope was no longer head of the Papal States, nor was he yet head of a Vatican City, which became a state only in 1929. In 1928 it was clear that the Pope would not again be the temporal ruler of an extensive state, but it was not yet clear in what sense if any he would be a temporal ruler. Dr. Garrison confronted a moot issue, but his tendency was to point out that the days of any significant temporal power for the Pope were over. The chief argument with which Dr. Garrison confronted his reader was not the weakening of the Pope's temporal power, but the growing evidence from American and other communities that Roman Catholics could indeed be loyal citizens to their native lands—and by now the majority of Roman Catholics in America were native born. With respect to the matter of a general allegiance to the United States Dr. Garrison gave its Roman Catholic citizens a clean bill of health. He then moved on from the general question to specific issues regarding which questions could be raised. The issue was not whether Roman Catholics should be accepted as loyal Americans until proven otherwise. The issue was, "Where does any particular Roman Catholic stand with respect to specific issues?" For instance, "How does a Roman Catholic understand the first amendment and its assertion that Congress shall make no laws regarding an establishment of religion?" or "What does a Roman Catholic believe about public support of parochial education?" or, for that matter, "What does a Roman Catholic believe about parochial education?" Dr. Garrison warned that while, on any such issue, certain tendencies were characteristic of the Catholic community, there was no stereotype, and the question must always be put in individual terms. In other words, the message of the book was that there is no reason why the fact that a man is a

Roman Catholic should, in and of itself disqualify him for the office of President of the United States.

The balance of his presentation increased the respect with which Dr. Garrison is held in the Roman Catholic community, and when in the 1960s the new ecumenical attitude inside Rome became public, Dr. Garrison was, in his city of Houston, quickly caught up into the Roman-Protestant dialogue in meetings, in radio-TV panels and in the press.

If Alexander Campbell is the symbol of debate with Rome, W. E. Garrison is the symbol of the discussion with Rome which is the prologue to the dialogue with Rome which is now taking shape.

The announcement by Pope John XXIII in 1959 that a general council of the Roman Catholic Church would soon be called was in itself a dramatic announcement. Such general or ecumenical councils have been held on the average of about once a century. After the First Vatican Council in 1870, many felt that another would never be called. The Council announced in 1959 was to be the 21st General Council, and soon it was disclosed that it would be held at the Vatican and would therefore be Vatican Council II. What happened in the next year, 1960, was even more dramatic. John XXIII announced that he would accept the invitation of the World Council of Churches to send observers to the forthcoming World Council Assembly in New Delhi (1961) and its Conference on Faith and Order at Montreal (1963). In turn, Protestant communions would be invited to send Delegated-Observers to Vatican Council II.

Confronting the multiplicity of Protestant communions, the Pope decided to issue his invitation to those communions which themselves had a world organization, that is, to those communions whose scope was such as to indicate that they had some appreciation of the concept of universality. The World Convention of Churches of Christ was approached, and, through its officers, accepted the invitation. For the first and second sessions the World Convention was assigned one place. During the first session it was filled by the late Dr. Jesse M. Bader, executive secretary of the World Convention of Churches of Christ. The position in the second session was occupied by Dr. W. G. Baker, a Church of Christ minister and scholar of Edinburgh, Scotland. During the third and fourth sessions the World Convention was assigned two places. W. B. Blakemore, Dean of the Disciples Divinity House of the University of Chicago served throughout those two sessions. In the third session the second place was filled for successive halves by Dr. W. G. Baker and Dr. Howard Elmo Short, editor of the *Christian*, St. Louis, Missouri. The second place during the fourth session was filled by Dr. Basil Holt, Church of Christ minister and missionary executive of Johannesburg, South Africa. By 1965 reports from these men, both in the press and personally had been made in Great Britain, America, Rhodesia, South Africa and Australia. These however are but the opening episodes of an ecumenical dialogue which will undoubtedly flourish in the future and for which concrete plans of various kinds are in the making.

What has already occurred so far as dialogue is concerned is that prior to the dramatic public announcements of John XXIII, and immediately thereafter, a fraternal spirit between Catholics and Disciples of Christ began at the grass roots level. In some areas it has not come into existence yet, and in one or two spots has withered back, for reasons of personality rather than for any reasons of principle. More frequently the ecumenical seed has sprouted and started a strong growth. Suspecting that this was the case, this writer in the summer of 1965 sent out letters to a sampling of Christian Church ministers across the United

States of America. Items selected from a few of the responses indicate the nature of what has been taking place.

One minister writes of the dramatic change in attitudes and activities of a catholic parish upon a change of rector. An older rector typified by older ways retired; a younger man coming in immediately urged his priests to become involved in community affairs along with the Protestant clergy of the mid-west college town where they all ministered. The young clerics were more than ready to become so involved. In Kansas City, for many months a group of Protestant and Catholic laymen "have had regular meetings and discussions of a very high level of churchmanship and theology." Disciples of Christ are included. Deane K. Lierle, pastor of the Christian Church in Monroe City, Missouri, has had "a regular relationship in the development of a community "prayer service" in which Protestant and Catholic clergy participate weekly."[58] In Tucson, Arizona, following the close of the first session of Vatican Council II the bishop of Tucson invited the clergy of all the churches to lunch and reported on the session. After the second session the other clergy gave the bishop a luncheon and heard his report.[59]

In Evansville, Indiana a "dialogue group" has been in existence about eight years—well before the calling of Vatican II. The group had its impetus from the National Council of Christians and Jews. At first the group discussed social issues, some of which were controversial; more recently it has turned to topics on the nature of the church and its ministry. Raphael H. Miller in his letter writes, "Two years ago at our Reformation Day services, sponsored by our Council of Churches, a Catholic priest was one of our speakers and gave a fine appreciation of Martin Luther.[60]

The ecumenical spirit was abroad in Portland, Oregon prior to Vatican Council II. Harold Glen Brown writes,

"Dr. William Cate of the Greater Portland Council of Churches began faith and order conversations with Catholics five or six years ago." Mr. Brown reports actions in 1960 by the Archbishop which were a very ready response to Protestant sensibilities when they were made known to him. Dr. Brown continues, "Since the Second Vatican Council we have had increasing cooperation . . . Some Catholics now belong to Committees of the Greater Portland Council of Churches . . . We have monthly faith and order conversations. We have had a public prayer service of Catholics, Protestants and Orthodox. The Catholics have now joined our ecumenical campus program at Portland State College and are paying $40,000 toward the cost of a new building . . . There have been local exchanges . . . For example Monsignor Tobin and I spoke in each other's churches at mid-week programs. I heard him tell his people to feel free to visit Protestant churches with spouses in the event of mixed marriages 'to strengthen the faith of the spouse who is Protestant.' "[61]

From Houston, Texas, Mr. Clarence Doss reports the rapidly growing accord which flourishes as ecumenically minded Protestants and the ecumenically minded Bishop Morkovsky work together on a variety of projects which widen and deepen Protestant-Catholic relationships.[62]

A most dramatic instance of Disciple involvement in the dialogue with Rome comes from Seattle, Washington. In 1964, the minister of University Christian Church there, Robert A. Thomas invited a local Catholic priest, a professor at Seattle University (a Jesuit institution), to teach a 13-week course on Protestant-Catholic relationships. It was reported in the press as the first such systematic teaching by a Catholic within the frame work of a Protestant Sunday school. "Whether it was or not," writes Mr. Thomas, "it certainly excited a considerable amount of attention locally and nationally." There was criticism within the congregation, and the state secretary of the Christian Churches, Mr. Van Doren, received a number of phone calls from Christian Church members who were quite critical, some of whom wanted him to put a stop to it. But, writes Mr. Thomas, "the end result of the experiment was good as far as most of our people were concerned . . . We plan to have another priest teach in our church school this winter." Meanwhile, as president of the Seattle Council of Churches, Mr. Thomas has been involved in a variety of Catholic-Protestant activities including the establishment of an Inter-Faith Ministerial Fellowship including Catholics, Protestants and Jews.[63]

Dr. Leslie R. Smith of Lexington, Kentucky writes: "There surely is a much warmer attitude. Our ecumenical service last October was held in Memorial Hall at the University, and a priest brought the evening sermon . . . At a wedding I just performed, Mrs. Smith discovered a Catholic priest in our Prayer Garden . . . He was killing time between buses . . . She invited him to the wedding— his first Protestant wedding and he went. He likewise went out to the reception with us and was greatly concerned. He was very open-minded, wanted to know my highest judgment of what was the weakest point in the Catholic faith, received the criticism very openly, and we had at least an hour's talk that was beneficial to us both . . . He said that the men who were being graduated as priests now were a completely different breed from him . . . he had always done what the Bishops and other officers asked him to do . . . he said that now the men were asking 'Why?' He admitted he was slipping into the same category."[64]

Following is a large part of a letter received from George R. Davis, minister of the National City Christian Church. What he writes arouses a faith that a Godly Providence may have been preparing the man who would one day become minister to the President of the United States, the

President who would succeed the martyred first Roman Catholic President. Mr. Davis writes:

"My contacts go back to the beginning of my ministry at the age of 16, and became well defined 30 years ago at the beginning of my first located pastorate after Seminary, at Chickasha. It is hard for me to believe how many people find modern ecumenical experiences new. I was having inter-faith services in Chickasha, Oklahoma, 30 years ago, with inter-faith prayer services, etc., and a kind of dialogue such as we know now.

"In St. Joseph, Missouri, 20 years ago we had such dialogues, etc. I was Chairman of an inter-faith service in the City Auditorium, with 10,000 attending, 300 in Choir, with Symphony Orchestra, singing Catholic, Jewish, Protestant hymns, and anthems; 60 priests, rabbis, ministers on platform. There was also a dramatic pageant, the Story of the Nation, related to religion. A Protestant guest speaker gave a brief sermon.

"In Wichita Falls I belonged to a dialogue group, and we had many inter-faith services. I was a member of the Advisory Board of the Catholic Hospital. Here in Washington I became a member of the original dialogue group in the nation following the Supreme Court Bible-prayer decision. We meet once each month. We have had several inter-faith services at National City, and of course for the Inaugural Service, we held the first such service of an inter-faith nature. I have been invited for three years to attend the Retreat, inter-faith, sponsored by the Jesuit Fathers, but conflicts in schedule have prevented each year.

"Perhaps my relationships have been too good for too many years to be of value in an accurate story. I have had the most frank relationships with priests, in discussions, etc., on every subject, etc. Of course the opening of the recent doors, on a broader scale do not seem strange to me, for my background prepared me for this. It may be I have been too open in my attitudes, and thus covered over serious problems beneath the surface. I do like to think I am aware of the serious problems, and never was deceived into thinking that more was being accomplished than was really being accomplished. But it has been a very rich experience across the years. Maybe I was just lucky in my background, my natural attitudes, etc., had the right parents, read the right books at the right time, for I have always felt at home with Roman Catholics, as well as Jewish Rabbis, and there has been no problem for me to get around to achieve the relationship."[65]

Participation through Delegated-Observers at Vatican Council II, but even more these reports from just a sampling of the ministry of the Christian Churches, indicate that indeed dialogue with Rome is well under way. At what points will this dialogue raise issues as the Christian Churches continue in their discovery of the church? To begin the discussion of our conclusions, let us return to the Campbell-Purcell debate.

We have already noted that Mr. Campbell announced himself as an advocate of order. Shortly thereafter Bishop Purcell drew from Campbell a statement which shows how far by 1837 Campbell had come from his *Christian Baptist* anti-clericalism of only a decade earlier. Did Mr. Campbell believe, asked Bishop Purcell, in any peculiar separation of any man or set of men for priestly functions—did he believe in the necessity of such call or mission.[66] Mr. Campbell affirmed that he did. Bishop Purcell then asked, "How is that calling made known, that mission given?" Campbell answered, "By the word and providence of God." "How can we ascertain that word and providence of God," asked Purcell. Campbell answered, "By the voice of the people and the written word—'vox populi vox Dei.'" The most crucial issues for the Christian Churches are involved in this encounter: particularly the nature of the church's ministry, and the relationship between the word and the church. The espousal by Alexander Campbell of the concept of *vox populi vox Dei* is in significant contrast to the position stated in *The Declaration and Address* where Thomas Campbell had written:

> A conscience that awaits the decision of the multitude, that hangs in suspense for the casting vote of the majority, is a fit subject for the man of sin. It is not the voice of the multitude, but the voice of truth, that has the power with the conscience—that can produce rational conviction, and acceptable obedience . . . Union in truth has been and ever must be, the desire and prayer of all such— Union in truth is our motto. The Divine Standard is our motto."[67]

These quotations from father and son indicate the dilemma for the Christian Churches—the Bible as the infallible rule and guide for faith and practice, or the voice of the people. There has been little evenness among the Christian Churches on this point. At times the Bible has been declared the highest authority, and at other times the highest authority has been declared to be the decisions of the congregation as a deliberative group. Dr. D. Ray Lindley emphasized what he believed was Campbell's recognition of the congregation as a deliberative group capable of reaching decision and action higher than that which its best minds, independently could have achieved.[68] Dr. Jesse Kellems has written:

> Campbell falls back upon a principle which is uniquely his own, his unswerving faith in the correct judgments of the enlightened common mind. In a word, the majority of those who love the Lord must always decide such questions, and the minority, as in all social compacts, must quietly bow to its will.[69]

Whether or not Kellems rightly interprets Campbell he has

here confused two concepts, namely "the common mind" and "the majority vote." They are not the same thing. The common mind is the mind common to all, and not just to the majority. The Christian Churches are among those in Christendom which have made extensive use of the majority vote. Actually it is not a heritage from the ancient church, but an importation from democratic government. The dialogue with Rome will raise questions for the Christian Churches regarding the use of majority votes. The decisions of Catholic councils are consensus, virtually unanimous decisions—just as are the decisions that come out of meetings of the Society of Friends.

We must point out however, that when Campbell responded to Purcell, he said, "By the voice of the people, and the written word—*vox populi vox Dei.*" In such a statement, Campbell is not proposing a Divine Standard which exists in abstraction. Though he may not have understood fully what he was indicating, he was indicating that the ultimate authority within Christianity belongs not to the Bible, but to the Bible within the church. Apart from the church the Bible has no authority. Even if we acknowledge a Divine authorship for the Bible, we must also acknowledge its formation within the matrix of the church, and whatever its accessibility to every faithful Christian, it can only be in congregation and not individually that its guidance for the religious community can be achieved. If the church of Christ is one church, dialogue with the Reformers would indicate that its order of ministry is an order that extends beyond the local congregation. Dialogue with the world indicates that the church must be understood as a human-divine institution. Dialogue with Rome brings us to the re-examination of the problem of biblical authority in terms of a Bible that is within the church, not outside or above it, but an authority made known by the voice of the people and the written word.

What must further be said is that while the Christian
churches have traditionally asserted that the Bible is the
ultimate authority, their practice has largely been that of
accepting as ultimate authority the voice of the churches
with the Bible in their midst. They probably would like
to effect what Campbell implies in the terms "the voice of
the people and the written word." To effect it they must
find some way of discovering the general voice of the communion. As benevolent, missionary and educational "societies" developed during the last century, "conventions"
developed. The conventions of several societies came to be
held on contiguous days. About the end of the 19th
century, by combining successive conventions, a general
Convention, advisory to the churches, was formed. The
authority of the Convention was enhanced a generation ago
by the formation within it of a Committee on Recommenda-
tions based on a delegate principle. At the present time,
at local, state and national levels, the Christian Churches
which use conventions to discover their common mind and
general character are exploring ways in which the delegate
principle may be more widely adopted—though in this move
toward delegate conventions they are cautiously watching
lest values in past procedures be inadvertently lost.

An authority in which the voice of the people and the
written word are combined is a lively, a living authority.
But a living authority moves forward in time, and it is a
point of reference, not in the past, not in some original
formulation of the Christian community, but in the present.
Only rarely in Christian Church history has this point been
noted. In 1888 a Disciple, J. W. Lowber wrote, "There is
a tendency among Protestants to disregard the authority of
the church . . . The Disciples believe the church is divine,
and that it is as important to obey the Bride as the Bride-
groom." Lowber may have been indulging in some wishful
thinking, for his is a lone voice in his time. More recently,

however, Disciple voices express a doctrine of the church in terms of a living church. This was the position taken by Dr. Charles Clayton Morrison in his Beecher Lecture of 1939 published under the title *What is Christianity*. In these lectures C. C. Morrison repudiated the notion that we see Christ only through the Bible. That actually was the position of the Campbells and of much other Reformed Protestantism. It is a position, declared Morrison, which takes Christ out of history. When we recapture the fact that the church is the Body of Christ we have again discerned Christ in history. Of Dr. Morrison's book W. Robinson of England wrote,

> If Harnack's book was the charter of Liberal Protestantism, Morrison's *What is Christianity* can be said to be a very real charter of Liberal Catholicism, and it comes as a challenge to the whole Protestant community, to whom it is chiefly addressed, to recognize both their failure and their true heritage.[70]

C. C. Morrison was certainly not a Roman Catholic, but he was leading his brethren in the direction of a Liberal Catholicism, that is, a recognition that it is the living church with the Bible in its midst that is the practically valid authority. This trend is typical not only of the Christian Churches but of Protestantism as a whole. Protestantism which in times past has emphasized the Bible alone, more and more acknowledges the Living Church as the only context within which the Bible can be validly interpreted and understood. There is remarkable evidence that Roman Catholicism, is, from the opposite direction coming toward Liberal Catholicism. Rome has exalted the authority of the Church, hierarchically conceived, often to the exclusion of the Bible. There is in this day a new Roman Catholicism, a new day of Biblical scholarship and an increasing day of the use of the Bible in Roman worship and familiarity with it by the laymen. Not only has the Mass with its several Scripture lessons now gone into English; recently it has been decided that priests should say or read the Daily Office in the vernacular. In conversation with a Roman priest in Rome in 1965, I commented that I thought the Roman Church might have preferred to keep the Daily Office in Latin, in order to preserve a wide-spread familiarity with Latin. The reply was, "It is more important for our minds, and therefore our mouths, to become filled with the English Bible—and it will happen because the Daily Office is largely Biblical in its content."

If Protestantism has been Bible apart from Church, Roman Catholicism has been Church apart from Bible—but a time of convergence seems to be at hand. Unity may be a long way off, but convergence is not to be ignored.

If convergence develops it will come about because men come within an understanding distance of each other—come into those attitudes and that spirit by which they listen to each other. Such a spirit is at work today. It must be present when a Christian Church survives having a Roman Catholic teach a Sunday school class, and when a Christian Church minister and a Catholic priest redeem the time killed between busses in conversation that proves beneficial to both. This is a new work of the Spirit in our day. Surely it is Holy Spirit at work, the spirit by which men stay within an understanding distance of each other. Thus it is the Spirit at work in the Assemblies of the World Council of Churches, and it is the Spirit by which Protestants and Catholics sit in each other's councils with such openness and candor that their respective prejudices are falling away, and they are rediscovering their common brotherhood in Christ. If this is Holy Spirit, it is Holy Spirit more powerfully effective in history than can be accounted for in any doctrine of the Spirit taught by Alexander Campbell. In the *Christian Baptist*[71] and again in the debate with N. L.

Rice, Campbell restricted the action of the Spirit to the influence of the biblical word. But when men will not listen to each other, the biblical word often enough divides them. There must first be that spirit by which men will *together* persist in searching the Scriptures that *they* may be led into truth. The Holy Spirit does not convey truth to men. It conveys men to each other in attitudes that enable them to seek the truth together. This is not Campbellite doctrine of the Holy Spirit. It is the Spirit at work in the world now which, by creating the spiritual conditions in which dialogue can occur, is leading Catholicism and Protestantism from opposite places toward a liberal catholicism.

If ultimately that conjunction into One Church is achieved, the men and women in it will be guided by the authority of a Living Voice reading with understanding the One Book within the One Church—and that this should be so, is Campbellite doctrine, and Christian Church doctrine, and Reformed doctrine, and Catholic doctrine—and the world's hope and the intention of God.

# IV

## *A Forward Look*

The encounters of the Disciples of Christ with the Reformers, the "world," and Roman Catholicism all began in the 19th century. These encounters were possible because of geographical propinquity. By the end of that century the Christian Churches had ventured on a missionary enterprise that was to bring their Brotherhood into relation with a variety of non-Christian religions, notably Hinduism in India, Buddhism in China and Japan, and primitive religions in Africa. Encounter with the non-Christian religions is, in our day, resulting in new understandings of mankind, including the personal and social consequences of his faiths. These encounters are contributing new understandings of the nature of religious community to the Disciples of Christ, and to Protestantism in general. There is a story to be told at some later time of the contributions that flow from the missionary endeavor into the Disciple discovery of the church.

Meanwhile the 20th century has witnessed the development of an ecumenical movement which has carried the Christian Churches into proximity to other Christian groups who in 1900 were remote and strange to the Disciples. Most notably, through the World Council of Churches, the Christian Churches have been brought into relationship with Orthodoxy, that form of Christianity which had its origins in the Greek speaking "Ancient East." Disciple contact with Orthodoxy accelerated immediately after World War II when the Disciples of Christ through the relief services of

96

the World Council of Churches had special responsibility for a traditionally Orthodox area of Eastern Europe. Subsequently there have been other contacts with Orthodoxy. While dialogue at depth is still to take place, in one very profound regard an Orthodox understanding of the church is already having influence upon Disciple ecclesiology. Disciples of Christ, like many other Protestants, are increasingly aware that Orthodoxy, for all its seeming traditionalism, has kept alive an appreciation of the eschatological dimension of the church which many newer communions have often ignored. Indeed, almost paradoxically, it is the oldest branch of Christendom which, by the preservation of eschatological thought is the most forward looking.

As the Disciples come more and more into relationship with Orthodoxy, they will increasingly comprehend the eschatological dimension of the church. The development of this dimension in Disciple consciousness goes on at present only episodically. The following illustration indicates the kind of experience which in this ecumenical age should become more frequent:

In July 1963 a half dozen Disciples of Christ were in Montreal attending the World Council of Churches' Fourth Conference on Faith and Order. On a Sunday morning arrangements had been made for these Disciples to attend an Orthodox service in the company of Dr. Nikos Nissiotis, a Greek, and a lay theologian of the staff of the World Council of Churches. The church building to which we went was new, modernistic in design, and architecturally very successful. The interior was flooded with bright light which came from a continuous band of window very high in the wall and just below the roof. The inner design brought attention to focus on the altar and its magnificant mosaic reredos. As the service began our group clustered around Dr. Nissiotis so that he could give us his comments. His first words were, "You must at all times remember that the attitude of the priest and the worshippers is that at Christ's altar we are standing in the future, at the edge of time and eternity, just prior to the heavenly feast of the lamb when we shall sit down together with our Lord in Glory."

As the Eucharistic liturgy proceeded, words and actions constantly called our minds forward to the contemplation of that moment when Christ breaks bread with his followers in the Heavenly Kingdom. Priest and congregation felt that they were at the very "gate of heaven," and the choir sang hymns in which they declared that they were symbolizing angelic and cherubic figures.

It was a startling experience for Disciples of Christ. In the celebration of the Lord's Supper in Christian Churches the emphasis is certainly that of looking back to the Upper Room. What is stressed in the Disciple communion service is remembrance. The most important words are the "words of institution" spoken by Christ himself or recorded for us by the apostles. At times we even seek to duplicate as closely as possible the actions of the original occasion. How startling then to realize that in the far older Orthodox body the aim of the liturgy has been, not to duplicate the original occasion of the Lord's Supper, but to approximate its ultimate occasion. While remembrance has some role, emphasis falls much more heavily on anticipation.

If we now bring to mind also the Roman Catholic Mass, it is striking to realize that in this service it is neither the original Last Supper nor the ultimate Feast of the Lamb that is the center of consciousness and emphasis. The emphasis is always on the present occasion of the Mass which involves the immediate presence of Christ. In times past Catholicism has stressed this immediacy in terms of a Real presence by virtue of a transubstantiation, discernible to faith, whereby the Eucharistic species of bread and wine become the body and blood of Christ. In more recent times

Catholics have emphasized equally if not more, various other ways in which Christ is present in relation to the Mass. All Protestants need to realize this recent expansion of the Catholic mind with regard to the presence of Christ. The decree on the Liturgy promulgated in 1963 by the Second Vatican Council has a paragraph which increasingly will open up the minds of Catholics—and indeed others—to the ways in which Christ is in our midst in worship.

. . . Christ is always present in his church, especially in her liturgical celebrations. He is present in the sacrifice of the Mass, not only in the person of his minister, "The same now offering, through the ministry of priest, who formerly offered himself on the cross," but especially under the Eucharistic species. By his power he is present in the sacraments, so that when a man baptizes it is really Christ himself who baptizes. He is present in his word, since it is he himself who speaks when the Holy Scriptures are read in the church. He is present, lastly, when the church prays and sings, for he promised: "Where two or three are gathered together in my name, there I am in the midst of them" (Matthew 18:20).

(From Section 7 of the Constitution on the Sacred Liturgy.)

Past. Present. Future. While each of these temporal dimensions is present in Reformed, Catholic and Orthodox worship, it is true that each of these three forms of worship has had a dominating emphasis: Reformed worship dominated by consciousness of the past, Catholic worship dominated by consciousness of the present, Orthodox worship dominated by consciousness of the future. Each needs the correction the other affords in order to discover the fulness of the church. In an ecumenical age the discovery of the church by the Disciples of Christ will include the discovery of its truly eternal character and its relationship to all time.

The membership of the church is always more than the living membership of any one congregation, or of all the presently existing congregations taken together. The membership of the church includes all the faithful who have gone before as well as those now living. The church is in communion with the saints and amid her present toils and tribulations she waits the consummation of that peace in which she will be the great church victorious.

And she on earth hath union with God the three in one,
And mystic sweet communion with those whose rest is won:
O happy ones and holy! Lord, give us grace that we,
Like them, the meek and lowly, on high may dwell with thee.

# NOTES

3369

1. See among other sources C. A. Young, *Historical Documents Advocating Christian Union* (Chicago: The Christian Century Company, 1904), p. 20.

2. See among other sources *Ibid.*, p. 73.

3. Typically within the Campbellite movement in accounting for unity the element of liberty has been overemphasized and the element of wide spread similarity in worship, doctrine and conduct have been greatly underemphasized. In recent generations as the similarity has been dissipated the idea of liberty has not proven enough to prevent the emergent dissimilarities in worship and behaviour from resulting in new groupings which amount to separate sects. There is no question that the "Church of Christ" (non-organ playing) does constitute such a sect. Opinions on both sides differ as to whether the "Disciples of Christ" and "The Christian Church" (Independents) have really become separate.

4. Young, *loc cit.*, p. 75.

5. *Ibid.*, p. 21.

6. *Ibid.*, p. 107.

7. *Ibid.*, p. 20.

8. *Ibid.*, p. 24.

9. Vachel Lindsay, "A Testament of Beauty," *Collected Poems* (New York: The Macmillan Co., 1931).

10. R. M. Pope, *The Church and Its Culture* (St. Louis: The Bethany Press, 1965).

11. N. L. Keith, *The Story of D. S. Burnet: Undeserved Obscurity* (St. Louis: The Bethany Press, 1954).

12. For a fuller analysis see W. B. Blakemore "The Issue of Polity for Disciples Today," esp. pp. 53-55, but *passim*, in W. B. Blakemore (ed.) *Revival of the Churches*, Vol. III, *The Renewal of Church: The Panel of Scholars Reports* (St. Louis: The Bethany Press, 1963), pp. 52-81.

13. A. T. DeGroot, *The Nature of the Church and Other Studies in Christian Unity* (Fort Worth, Texas: Published by the author, Texas Christian University, 1961), p. 14.

14. Alexander Campbell, *The Christian System,* 3rd edition (Pittsburgh: Forrester and Campbell, 1840, printed at Bethany, West Virginia by A. Campbell), chap. XXIV.

15. Alexander Campbell and N. L. Rice, *A Debate on the Action, Subject, Design and Administration of Christian Baptism* (Lexington, Kentucky: A. T. Skillman and Sons, 1844).

16. F. D. Kershner, *How to Promote Christian Union* (Cincinnati, Ohio: The Standard Publishing Company, 1916), chaps. I-VIII.

17. *Ibid.*, chaps. VIII-XII.

18. *The Sacred Writings* (Cover title—*The New Testament*) (Buffaloe, Brooke County, Virginia: Printed and published by A. Campbell, 1826).

19. Alexander Campbell, *A Connected View of the Principles and Rules by Which the Living Oracles May be Intelligibly and Certainly interpreted.* For full bibliographical reference see under "A Campbell" in C. E. Spencer, *An Author Catalog of Disciples of Christ* (Canton, Missouri: Disciples of Christ Historical Society, 1946), p. 49, column 3.

20. W. B. Blakemore (ed.) *The Renewal of Church: The Panel of Scholars Reports* (St. Louis, Missouri: The Bethany Press, 1963), 3 vols., *passim*, but see especially Vol. II, R. G. Wilburn (ed.) *The Reconstruction of Theology* Part I, "Bible and Tradition for the Faith Today" for papers by Baird, England, Hyatt and Williams.

21. C. C. Morrison, *The Meaning of Baptism* (Chicago: Disciples Publication Society, 1914).

22. A position elaborated at length by C. C. Morrison forty years later in his book *The Unfinished Reformation* (New York: Harper and Brothers, 1953), esp. pp. 166-174.

23. *Christian Baptism* (Doctrines of the Christian Faith: Study Report No. 3), prepared by the Study Committee of the World Convention of Churches of Christ (Disciples), (St. Louis: Christian Board of Publication, 1956), p. 5.

24. Jack Finegan, *First Steps in Theology* (New York: The Association Press 1960), p. 88.

25. J. P. Hyatt, "The Origin and Meaning of Christian Baptism," R. G. Wilburn (ed.) *The Reconstruction of Theology*, p. 279.

26. *Ibid.*, p. 285.

27. D. E. Stevenson, *The Church—What—Why*, Christian Discipleship Series, Basic Course I (St. Louis: Christian Board of Publication, 1962), pp. 53 ff.

28. *Ibid.*, p. 54.

29. W. B. Blakemore, *The Cornerstone and the Builders*, Christian Foundation Lectures, delivered in Emmanuel College, University of Toronto, January 1955. Published by the College of the Church of Christ in Canada see pp. 15 ff., and esp. pp. 34-37.

30. L. G. McAllister, *Thomas Campbell: Man of the Book* (St. Louis: The Bethany Press, 1954), pp. 39-44.

31. Young, *loc cit.*, p. 71.

32. *Ibid.* p. 86.

33. *Ibid.*, p. 80.

34. J. T. Barclay, *The City of the Great King* (Philadelphia: James Challen and Sons, 1858).

35. For an extended discussion of the topics of this section see H. L. Lunger, *The Political Ethics of Alexander Campbell* (St. Louis: The Bethany Press, 1954).

36. *Ibid.*, p. 48.

37. Alexander Campbell and Robert Owen, *Debate on the Evidences of Christianity* (Bethany, West Virginia: Alexander Campbell, 1829).

38. Young, *loc. cit.*, p. 75.

39. When this chapter was delivered as a lecture on November 9, 1965, at this point the following comment was made: "We need to be clear about this matter. In this year of 1965 when the Second Vatican Council promulgates its declaration on Religious Liberty, the principle of voluntaryism in its two legitimate meanings will be acknowledged by the Roman Catholic Church. The declaration to be made will affirm the principle that the state must regard all religious communities as voluntary associations of believers. More important is the fact that the declaration will affirm that the individual conscience cannot be forced. As a Protestant heir of Locke's *Treatise on Civil Government*, I will rejoice that such a declaration of Religious Liberty is made. But I am equally glad that long ago, while I was confirmed in the significance of the concept of voluntary association as political doctrine, and as a teaching in regard to the individual Christian, I

was disabused of attempts to make it the fundamental point in a doctrine of the church."

40. E. S. Ames, *Religion* (New York: Henry Holt and Co., 1929), p. 271.
41. *Ibid.*, p. 282.
42. *Ibid.*, p. 280.
43. W. B. Blakemore, *The Liberal Era Among the Disciples of Christ.* The W. E. Garrison Lectures for 1964 (unpublished), delivered at The Disciples House, New Haven, Connecticut.
44. C. E. Lemmon, *The Art of Church Management* (St. Louis: The Bethany Press, 1933).
45. O. L. Shelton, *The Church Functioning Effectively* (St. Louis, Christian Board of Publication, 1946).
46. E. S. Ames, *The Psychology of Religious Experience* (New York: Houghton-Mifflin Co., 1910).
47. Angus Dun, *Prospecting for a United Church* (New York: Harper and Bros., 1948).
48. McAllister, *loc. cit.*, pp. 21-59.
49. Young, *loc. cit.* p. 86.
50. This period in Campbell's career is definitively portrayed in R. F. West, *Alexander Campbell and Natural Religion* (New Haven, Connecticut: Yale University Press, 1946), Chap II, pp. 7-28.
51. W. E. Garrison, *Heritage and Destiny* (St. Louis: The Bethany Press, 1961), p. 40.
52. Alexander Campbell and J. B. Purcell, *A Debate on the Roman Catholic Religion* (Cincinnati, Ohio: J. A. James and Co., 1837).
53. *Ibid.*, p. 40.
54. *Ibid.*, p. 28.
55. *Ibid.*, p. 33.
56. *Ibid.*, p. 357.
57. W. E. Garrison, *Catholicism and the American Mind* (Chicago: Willett, Clark and Colby, 1928).
58. From letter written by K. A. Kuntz, minister First Christian Church, Hannibal, Missouri, August 9 1965.
59. From letter written by J. R. Moffett, minister First Christian Church, Tucson, Arizona, September 3 1965.
60. From letter written by R. H. Miller, Jr., minister East Side Christian Church, Evansville, Indiana August 21, 1965.
61. From letter written by H. G. Brown, minister First Christian Church, Portland, Oregon, August 23, 1965.
62. From letter written by C. M. Doss, minister Heights Christian Church, Houston, Texas, September 14, 1965.
63. From letter written by R. A. Thomas, minister University Christian Church, Seattle, Washington, August 6, 1965.
64. From letter written by L. R. Smith, minister Central Christian Church, Lexington, Kentucky, August 30, 1965.
65. From letter written by G. R. Davis, minister National City Christian Church, Washington, D. C., September 4, 1965.
66. Campbell and Purcell *loc. cit.*, p. 44.
67. Young, *loc. cit.*, p. 116.
68. D. Ray Lindley, "The Structure of the Church," R. E. Osborn (ed.), *The Reformation of Tradition*, Vol. I, *The Renewal of Church*, pp. 188 ff.
69. Quoted in A. T. DeGroot, *The Nature of the Church*, p. 19.
70. *Ibid.*, p. 18.

71. Alexander Campbell, "Essays on the Work of the Holy Spirit," pp. 82, 89, 95, 101, 108, 117, 124, 131 and 137 in *The Christian Baptist*, 15th ed. St. Louis: Christian Publishing Co.

For all writings prior to 1946 by Disciple of Christ authors, definitive bibliographical information is available in Claude E. Spencer, *An Author Catalog of Disciples of Christ* (Canton, Missouri: Disciples of Christ Historical Society, 1946).